INTERNATIONAL THEMES AND ISSUES

VOLUME 2

THE SHOCK OF WAR

INTERNATIONAL THEMES AND ISSUES

A joint series of the Canadian Historical Association
and the University of Toronto Press

SERIES EDITOR | Beverly Lemire

INTERNATIONAL THEMES AND ISSUES
A joint series of the Canadian Historical Association
and the University of Toronto Press

SERIES EDITOR | Beverly Lemire

THE SHOCK OF WAR
Civilian Experiences, 1937–1945

SEAN KENNEDY

University of Toronto Press

Library and Archives Canada Cataloguing in Publication

Kennedy, Sean, 1969–
    The shock of war : civilian experiences, 1937–1945 / Sean Kennedy.

Includes bibliographical references and index.
Also issued in electronic formats.
ISBN 978-1-4426-0370-7

    1. World War, 1939–1945—Social aspects.   2. Civilians in war—History—20th
century.   3. World War, 1939–1945—Atrocities.   4. War and society—History—
20th century.   I. Title.

D744.6.K45 2010   940.53'1   C2010-907767-9

We welcome comments and suggestions regarding any aspect of our publications—please
feel free to contact us at news@utphighereducation.com or visit our Internet site at
www.utppublishing.com.

North America
5201 Dufferin Street
North York, Ontario,
Canada, M3H 5T8

2250 Military Road
Tonawanda, New York,
USA, 14150

ORDERS PHONE: 1-800-565-9523
ORDERS FAX: 1-800-221-9985
ORDERS E-MAIL: utpbooks@utpress.utoronto.ca

UK, Ireland, and continental Europe
NBN International
Estover Road, Plymouth, PL6 7PY, UK
ORDERS PHONE: 44 (0) 1752 202301
ORDERS FAX: 44 (0) 1752 202333
ORDERS E-MAIL: enquiries@nbninternational.com

The University of Toronto Press acknowledges the financial support for its publishing
activities of the Government of Canada through the Canada Book Fund.

Printed in Canada

Contents

Acknowledgements

This short book took me considerably longer than expected to complete. I am now very pleased to thank the people who have made its publication possible.

Since this is a work of synthesis, I must first acknowledge the efforts and talents of the vast number of scholars who have written on the subject. I have tried to indicate my intellectual debts more precisely in the references and in the suggestions for further reading. I hope that I have not misrepresented the views of any author. I must also thank the staff of the Harriet Irving Library, especially its Document Delivery Department. They procured a wide range of works for me cheerfully and speedily.

I am extremely grateful to Beverly Lemire for first drawing my attention to the International Themes and Issues Series. She has been consistently encouraging and provided very helpful commentary on the draft manuscript. The anonymous reviewers who commented on my proposal for the book, and the two readers who subsequently assessed the manuscript itself, performed these roles with great professionalism and provided many perceptive suggestions. They helped me to sharpen my ideas and saved me from a number of errors. Two of my colleagues in the University of New Brunswick's Department of History, Marc Milner and Lisa Todd, also read the entire draft manuscript; I sincerely appreciate their willingness to take on this task, and the detailed suggestions that they provided.

Throughout the publication process, first with Broadview Press and now with the Higher Education Division of the University of Toronto Press,

Natalie Fingerhut has been a model editor. She has responded promptly to my ongoing queries, provided clear and constructive suggestions, and was both patient and supportive when personal and professional obligations resulted in delays. Betsy Struthers has sharpened the writing with skilled and efficient copy editing: I thank her for saving me from a number of mistakes and clarifying my ideas at critical points. Beate Schwirtlich has been an enthusiastic and supportive production coordinator, encouraging me through the final stages of editing. My thanks go to Anna Del Col for her efforts in marketing the book and for keeping me informed about the splendid work done by the cover designer. In sum, the entire UTP Higher Education team has been a delight to work with. Of course, whatever short-comings the book retains are my responsibility.

My wife Lisa has been an enthusiastic supporter of this project from its inception. She encouraged me to write for a broader audience, and provided both practical suggestions and unconditional encouragement as I worked. It may seem inappropriate to dedicate a book that explores suffering on such a massive scale to anyone, but I want to recognize how much she has helped me, in so many ways.

Introduction

A family is shattered by the loss of a father or son in battle. A young woman seizes new opportunities, and confronts new challenges, after she leaves her old job to work in a munitions plant. A merchant faces the difficult choice of whether or not to sell to German or Japanese occupiers. A community is devastated by aerial bombardment, with the threat of more looming ahead. These are only some of the myriad experiences of civilians during the Second World War. This book seeks to analyze those experiences, notably the pressures imposed by the demands of mobilization; the challenges of living under foreign occupation; the many atrocities visited upon non-combatants; and the social, political, and psychological impact of the most intense and destructive conflict the modern world has ever seen.

No war has ever spared civilians, but the advent of "total wars" in the era spanning from the French Revolution to the Second World War entailed growing civilian involvement and often greater civilian suffering. In total wars massive armed forces are committed to battle, economies are geared heavily towards military demands, and war aims become increasingly ambitious. The demand made on civilians for material and moral support, and the extent to which they are exposed to destruction, expand. During the French Revolutionary and Napoleonic Wars of 1792–1815 states brought large male populations under arms, while requiring those behind the front line to sacrifice in terms of labour, financial contribution through taxation, and conformity to national war aims. After 1815 the wars fought in Europe were generally limited in duration and more restrained in the demands on non-combatants, but the American Civil War of 1861–65 gave some indication of what lay ahead. Both North and South organized huge armies and mobilized their populations. The destruction wrought upon civilians was extensive, and communities and families were often bitterly divided by this internal conflict. The war also served as a catalyst for profound social change, above all the abolition of slavery, though the expectations of many African Americans were, ultimately, cruelly disappointed.

It was the civilian experience of the First World War, however, that most directly pre-figured that of the Second. All governments, both those of the Triple Entente of the British Empire and its Dominions, France and its colonial empire, and the Russian Empire—joined by Italy in 1915 and the United States in 1917—and the Central Powers, consisting of Germany, Austria-Hungary, and the Ottoman Empire, devoted ever-greater resources to the war effort. The growing proportion of young men at the front drew new workers, many of them women, into the labour force. Governments encouraged financial contributions through measures such as bond campaigns and rationed various items, often with increasing rigour. Civilians found news about the conflict filtered by censorship and propaganda. Government departments, as well as newspapers and journalists acting on their own accord, stressed the need for loyalty and encouraged hatred of the enemy.

The experiences of civilians in 1914–18 were extremely diverse, but some general trends can be noted. The millions of people who entered war work had to adjust to the rigours of factory production. While many experienced significant wage increases and a greater degree of financial independence, conditions were harsh, even dangerous, especially in munitions facilities. Those who lived in rural areas faced various regulations and requisitions, even if they sometimes had more regular access to food. By the later years of the war some countries were experiencing a "food crunch"; rationing stretched the patience of those on the home front to the limit. Inflation was a significant problem in many countries, as those on fixed incomes, including pensioners and many civil servants, found their purchasing power drastically reduced.

By and large, people on the home fronts during the First World War were initially supportive of their governments, but as the conflict wore on tensions mounted. Conditions were harsher in some countries than others, but one common complaint was that sacrifices were not being equally shared. In many states, various observers feared that the growing numbers of women in the workforce would weaken the family and that the strains of war were encouraging lax sexual mores and juvenile delinquency. Intensified nationalism and heightened vigilance led to a generalized suspicion of foreigners, minorities, and dissenters. By 1916–17 there was growing disaffection in several countries. The situation was most dramatic in the Russian Empire, where worsening conditions and frustration at the government's ineptitude led to the collapse of the Tsarist regime. In Germany, where food shortages were quite serious, strikes and protests initially focused on this issue but quickly took on a political dimension. In France foreign workers, many of them from the colonies, faced racist violence. This stemmed partly from fears by local men that the newcomers would take their jobs and lure away French women.

Millions of civilians also faced the terrifying realties of conflict and the grim experience of foreign occupation. Cities such as London, Paris, and Karlsruhe were bombed from the air, while many populations were exposed to frequent artillery shelling. Occupation could take a heavy toll. For example, the German army occupied vast territories in Eastern Europe, as well as much of Belgium and northern France. In all of these regions populations endured requisitions of material and labour. Occupying troops sometimes engaged in killing non-combatants; as many as 6,000 Belgian and French civilians, for example, were killed by invading German troops. The largest scale wartime massacre of non-combatants, the slaughter of approximately 1 million Armenians by the Ottoman Army, took place in a different context, in which the government accused a long-persecuted minority of conspiring with the enemy. The mass killing of the Armenians illustrates the extent to which the line dividing civilians from combatants could dissolve, especially when wartime suspicions built upon earlier hatreds.

The experiences of the First World War help us to comprehend what happened during the Second. They highlight the extent to which civilian and military experiences were intertwined, even by things as simple as ongoing correspondence between soldiers and their families. They underscore the growing role of the state in managing economies and morale. They show how vulnerable civilians could be both to rapidly evolving military technologies and to atrocities. They indicate how mobilization could reconfigure society, whether in the realm of gender relations, the status of youth, attitudes about race, or frictions between different classes.

To be sure, some of the changes associated with the war were temporary. After the guns silenced, in countries like Britain and France rationing gradually gave way to more normal consumption patterns, propaganda campaigns wound down, and for the lucky ones physical separation came to an end. Moreover, in some cases wartime developments reinforced already existing social trends. The changing role of women in Western society, for instance, was a subject of controversy well before 1914. The mark of war upon millions of people was permanent, whether it meant losing a loved one or meeting a future spouse. Societies and nations were also lastingly scarred, and major social and political upheavals persisted long after the 11 November 1918 armistice. Opposition to war helped to fuel the Bolshevik Revolution of 1917, which was followed by years of civil war. There were labour protests and upheavals over much of the globe in 1918–19, and the collapse of the German, Austro-Hungarian, and Ottoman Empires turned out to be a protracted, often bloody process.

Notwithstanding initial hopes that the cataclysm of 1914–18 would be "the war to end all wars," the ensuing decades of the 1920s and especially the 1930s were fraught with tension. Hopes for peaceful international cooperation, embodied in the creation of the League of Nations, unravelled. Persisting nationalist tensions were crucial to this process; so was a troubled world economy devastated by the Great Depression, which began in the United States in 1929 but soon affected much of the globe. International trade plummeted, unemployment soared, and extremist doctrines gained appeal. By the mid-1930s a growing number of politicians, especially in Europe, were convinced that another war was on the horizon. Denis Brogan, a British historian, observed in January 1936 that "We all stand in the shadow of a great fear, and if the angel of death is not yet abroad in the land, we can hear the beating of his wings—and see them too, filling our old familiar sky."[1] Brogan, and many others, grew increasingly worried because expansionist policies on the part of Imperial Japan, Fascist Italy, and above all Nazi Germany threatened, and eventually brought about, a new global conflict.

Though Japan had begun empire-building in the late nineteenth century, seizing control of Taiwan (then Formosa) in 1895 and Korea in 1910, during the 1920s its leaders adopted a cooperative approach in dealing with Western nations. When Japan was hit hard by the Great Depression, this outlook was discredited. Traditional government structures remained in place, but ultra-nationalists, within and outside the military, increasingly dominated them. The nationalists encouraged the militarization of Japanese society and promoted renewed colonial expansion as the solution to the country's economic problems. In September 1931, the Kwantung Army invaded the Chinese province of Manchuria. While the government in Tokyo had not ordered this act of aggression, it quickly sanctioned it, and in 1932 the conquered province became the Japanese puppet state of Manchukuo. Though not yet engaging in a full-scale mobilization of the Japanese people, the government and much of Japan's media promoted the conquest enthusiastically. They encouraged mass migration to Manchukuo, presenting it as an example of how Asian societies with the fraternal support of Japan could be modernized and freed from the evils of Soviet Communism and Western imperialism. In reality Manchukuo was in all but name a Japanese colony, where the local population experienced subjugation. The conquest turned out to be a key step in an empire-building campaign that the Japanese people were increasingly required to support.

As Japan renewed its expansion in Asia, Fascist Italy began empire-building in the Mediterranean in an attempt to recapture the power and glory of the Roman era. Benito Mussolini, who had been the country's prime minister and then dictator since 1922, pursued a generally cautious foreign policy during his first 10 years in power, but thereafter the militaristic character of his regime became more evident. *Il Duce* did not hide his belief that the Italian people—Italian men, at least—should be more vigorous and warlike. In 1932 he ordered that plans be drawn up to seize control of Ethiopia. The African country was believed to have mineral and oil resources and could be a valuable site for Italian migration. Revenge was another powerful motive, however, for Ethiopian troops had previously humiliated the Italians at the Battle of Adowa in 1896. In October 1935 Fascist Italy launched a full-scale invasion. Using aerial bombardment and poison gas against Ethiopian civilians as well as its armed forces, they proclaimed victory in May 1936. While drawing some international criticism, Mussolini's colonial adventure generated enthusiasm at home, reinforcing his belief that imperial expansion would buttress his domestic support and remould Italian society along more Fascist lines. He continued on this path in the years that followed, even though constant military activity was an enormous burden for the Italian economy and Italians were often less than enthusiastic about their nation's deepening alliance with Nazi Germany.

Destructive though Fascist expansionism was, it was the foreign policy of Nazi Germany that ultimately led to the outbreak of the Second World War in Europe. While Japanese nationalists sought to dominate Asia and Mussolini wanted a Fascist Mediterranean empire, Hitler's primary target for expansion was Eastern Europe, which held not only resources but also *Lebensraum* (living space) for German colonization. Hitler realized that Western Europe could not be ignored. Germany's historic enemy, France, had to be subdued, and while Hitler talked about working with the British, if they refused he would not tolerate them standing in his way. However, in the Nazi leader's profoundly racist world view, the chief obstacles to his goals were the Slavic peoples of Eastern Europe and, above all, the Jews. Hitler and his lieutenants saw Slavs as inferior beings to be relocated, or decimated, as required; the rest were destined to serve the Germans. As for Jews, the Nazis regarded them as a deadly racial and political threat. Within Germany itself they were an inherently subversive element that had to be neutralized. In Europe, especially in the East, they were the agents of Communism and racial degeneration.

Hitler initially displayed some caution after taking power in 1933, but it did not take very long for his regime's militarist and racist character, or its expansionist impulses, to emerge. As early as 1934 he supported a failed Nazi coup attempt in Austria. In 1935 Germany proclaimed that it was rearming, in defiance of the postwar peace settlement. In 1938 Hitler, declaring that he wanted to gather the Germans into one state, began to acquire territories by the threat of force. Austria was incorporated into the Reich in March 1938. In September of that year, following months of pressure and the threat of a European war, Britain and France pressed Czechoslovakia to cede its Sudeten region, where the majority of the population was German, to the Nazis. In contrast to Italy and Japan, Germany did not engage in a shooting war to take these territories, but the country's aggressive intentions were clear, both abroad and at home. The Nazi regime undertook a massive rearmament campaign and heavily promoted military values through organizations such as the Hitler Youth. The Reich also persecuted political opponents, potential dissidents, and ethnic minorities, especially the Jews. The Nuremberg Laws stripped them of their civil rights in 1935; in the years that followed they endured further racist restrictions, the confiscation of their property, and, as demonstrated by a nationwide pogrom in November 1938, growing physical violence. Though Hitler did not have a "blueprint" with respect to foreign or racial policy, Germany's internal and external policies made war increasingly likely.

During the second half of the 1930s Fascist Italy and Nazi Germany became allies, as demonstrated by their intervention in the Spanish Civil War of 1936–39. The conflict in Spain, between the elected, left-leaning government of the Spanish Republic and the right-wing nationalist rebels led by General Francisco Franco, supported by Fascist Italy and Nazi Germany, was rooted in that country's particular social and political divisions. But the struggle also reflected broader ideological conflicts in Europe. Both the Republican Loyalists and Franco's Nationalists mobilized the civilian populations in the regions of Spain they controlled, and both sides committed atrocities against non-combatants. Franco in particular was determined to "purify" Spain through a campaign of systematic repression, which continued long after he achieved victory in 1939. Atrocities of this sort presaged the destruction caused by ideologically charged repression during the Second World War. Events such as the destruction of the town of Guernica by German aircraft in April 1937, as well as repeated attacks on other cities like Madrid, provided a further frightening reminder of the vulnerability of civilians.

Hitler and especially Mussolini committed major resources and personnel in support of Franco's Nationalists, partly to test their own armed forces, partly for ideological and strategic reasons. Their intervention ensured Franco's victory. As for the Spanish Republicans, the only major power who came to their aid was the Soviet Union, whose foreign policy during the 1930s followed a complex course. Established by the Bolshevik Revolution of 1917, the Soviet Union was under the dictatorial rule of Joseph Stalin by the 1930s. Stalin's diplomacy reflected ideological influences but also ruthless pragmatism. From its inception the Soviet Union had declared itself in favour of international Communist revolution, and during the early 1930s it was often a harsh critic of Western democracies, notably Britain, France, and the United States, who had supported the Bolsheviks' enemies in the Russian Civil War of 1918–21. Following Hitler's rise to power, however, Stalin shifted his approach in response to aggressive Nazi anti-Communism. From 1934 the Soviet Union publicly emphasized its opposition to fascism and promoted "collective security," whereby the Soviets and the Western democracies would cooperate to oppose expansionist nations like Germany. Soviet intervention in the Spanish Civil War arguably represented the high-water mark of Stalin's anti-fascist foreign policy, though the Spanish Republicans had to pay for Soviet help, and for reasons that are still debated Stalin did not commit sufficient resources to turn the tide.

While Soviet foreign policy followed a complex course during the 1930s, at home Stalin made his people endure a wrenching effort to transform the country into an industrial giant through the mechanism of a centralized, state-run economy. This was the only way, he insisted, to prevent the country from being overwhelmed by the capitalist states. His officials subjected Soviet citizens to military-style discipline in the workplace and urged them to exceed their work quotas. Most private farms were consolidated into large state-run collectives, frequently through coercion. Those who stood, or were perceived to be standing, in Stalin's way—which turned out to be millions of people—faced repression, internment, and often death. By the eve of the Second World War the Soviet Union was indeed a major industrial power, but its population had been traumatized. In addition to the repression associated with his economic policies, Stalin had also overseen a series of purges that decimated the ranks of the Communist Party and the Soviet officer corps. In the long run, the economic changes of the 1930s helped give the Soviet Union the industrial base it would need to resist the German invasion launched in 1941. However, the mass repression of that decade devastated its military leadership, left elements of the population severely disaffected, and rendered Stalin desperate to avoid war with Hitler.

The leading Western democracies—Britain, France, and the United States—did not intervene in the Spanish Civil War. This was in keeping with their strong desire to avoid war during the 1930s, for a variety of reasons. Britain and France had little reason to disturb the international status quo. Victors in the First World War, both had vast empires and were determined to preserve their standing in an uncertain world. Both also struggled to recover from the Great Depression, and until 1939 it seems each perceived itself to be at a disadvantage, in terms of military preparations, in relation to Germany. The horrors of 1914–18 were fresh in the minds of British politicians, as well as the leaders of the dominions of Canada, Australia, and New Zealand. In France, where First World War losses had been even higher, the will to avoid further bloodshed was at least as strong.

The case of the United States was somewhat different. The United States' participation in the First World War had been shorter in duration (1917–18), and the conflict had a less traumatic impact on the national psyche. The United States felt safer because of its geographic location. Moreover, in the late 1930s it was still struggling with economic troubles, and in military terms it was well behind the European powers. President Franklin Roosevelt worried about the expansion of Japanese and German power, but he was very sensitive to the powerful current of isolationism in US society. Many US politicians and citizens felt that their country's involvement in the First World War had been a grave mistake and were now strongly opposed to getting involved in the affairs of Europe in particular. Roosevelt himself opposed German, Italian, and Japanese plans; he tried to get Congress and the people to follow his lead, but the United States did not actually enter the war until Japan attacked Pearl Harbor on 7 December 1941, over two years after the fighting had begun in Europe.

The desire to avoid war led the Western democracies, above all Britain and France, to pursue a policy of appeasement—preserving peace through conciliating Germany. The policy is most closely associated with British Prime Minister Neville Chamberlain, but he was supported, albeit sometimes reluctantly, by French Prime Minister Édouard Daladier. Though both leaders also pursued rearmament, appeasement remained their dominant approach until 1939. The most notorious incident was the Czechoslovak crisis, which culminated in France and Britain sacrificing the Sudetan territory to Germany in order to avoid war. Although the Munich Accords that finalized this deal were accompanied by a sense of relief, a growing element of the British and French elite and public opinion felt ashamed of abandoning the Czechs and Slovaks. Before long, it was clear that appeasement was failing. In March 1939 Hitler ordered his military to occupy the Czech lands of Bohemia and Moravia, while Slovakia was transformed into a German puppet state. The Nazi leader also began to demand the cession of the city of Danzig, a predominantly German-speaking community, from Poland.

Though fears of war remained, public opinion in Britain and France increasingly felt that Hitler had to be confronted: it seemed clear that he was set upon dominating Europe and that his demands could not be satisfied. Given the fact that both Britain and France ruled over colonial empires in which non-whites lacked rights, and would soon be required to support a major war effort without having a say in the matter, their criticisms of Nazi expansionism and racism might seem compromised today. But, as historian Richard Overy notes, both countries believed they were the upholders of Western liberal democratic values that were now imperilled. In 1939, as their economies recovered, and as their intelligence services indicated that they were militarily better prepared to confront Germany, Chamberlain and Daladier grew more assertive. In March 1939 the British declared that they would support Poland's defiance of German claims upon Danzig; France, already an ally of Poland, concurred.

Amidst a growing sense of crisis in the spring and summer of 1939, there was much speculation about what Stalin would do. Since 1934 the Soviet Union had publicly declared its opposition to fascism, stressing the need for international cooperation. But most British and French politicians and military officials balked at working with the Soviets. They were deeply suspicious of Stalin and feared that he would exploit the international situation to promote revolution and overthrow capitalism. By 1939 the situation was dire enough that they now engaged in talks with him. If the Soviet Union aligned with Britain and France, Germany would have enemies to the east and the west and thereby might be deterred. However, the negotiations dragged along, amidst a climate of suspicion on both sides.

In fact, by this time the Soviets were secretly negotiating with the Germans, who believed that if they could secure Soviet cooperation, Britain and France might back down from their guarantee to Poland. The Nazi-Soviet negotiations led to the announcement, on 23 August 1939, that the two nations had signed a non-aggression pact. Given the sharp ideological differences between the Soviet Union and the Reich, how can this be explained? In some respects, the answer is simple. Stalin still distrusted the British and French, who could offer little beyond a good chance of having to go to war with Germany. By contrast, the Nazis offered not only the chance to avoid war but to gain territory as well. Indeed, the Nazi-Soviet agreement included secret provisions for Germany and the Soviet Union to divide most of Eastern Europe between them. Finally, Stalin was aware that his purges had gravely weakened his country; the longer he could avoid a confrontation with Germany, the better.

As Stalin saw it, signing the agreement was in his self-interest. Doing so also greatly enhanced the chances for a war, because now Hitler felt that he could move against Poland without having to be concerned about Soviet opposition (Stalin's decision also placed the Soviet Union in a much more vulnerable position relative to Germany, as became apparent in 1941). Hitler now hoped that the British and the French, having failed to woo the Soviets, would back down, but they would not. On 1 September 1939, German forces crossed the Polish frontier; Britain and France declared war two days later.

Millions of people had feared a repetition of the cataclysm of 1914–18. What followed exceeded the worst nightmares of many, for the Second World War proved to be longer and more widespread than its predecessor. In 1914–18 the fighting was concentrated in Europe, with significant engagements in the Middle East and smaller ones in Africa and East Asia. By contrast, the Second World War engulfed most of Asia and Europe. The conflict also spread to the Mediterranean, Africa, and finally to the Pacific following the attack on Pearl Harbor. In general civilians were more fully involved and suffered more widely. In many countries they were called upon to make great sacrifices, and in numerous occupied regions and battle zones they endured hunger, maltreatment, atrocities, and even genocide. Recent estimates suggest that as many as 60 million people lost their lives during the Second World War, more than double that of the First; the majority of those people were civilians.

What follows attempts to convey something of the diverse challenges, experiences, and horrors that ordinary people in various countries experienced during the Second World War. Chapter 1 examines how dictatorships and democracies tried, in very different ways and with different results, to galvanize their populations in support of the war effort, and the social and political implications of, and tensions caused by, wartime mobilization. Chapter 2 considers what it was like for people to live under foreign occupation, through an examination of the wartime empires created by Nazi Germany and Imperial Japan. We will see how civilians were forced to adapt to various restrictions and shortages, and the kinds of personal and political choices they made in a dangerous and uncertain world. Violence against civilians is the subject of Chapter 3; it explores the varying reactions and fates of non-combatants caught in the path of invading armies, killed by aerial bombardments, or targeted for murder because of their ethnic background. Chapter 4 surveys the aftermath of the war, considering the ways in which the conflict transformed the societies that had been engulfed by it.

Further Reading

For broader perspectives, see Arthur Marwick, *War and Social Change in the Twentieth Century* (London: Macmillan, 1974); Gabriel Kolko, *Century of War: Politics, Conflicts, and Society since 1914* (New York: The New Press, 1994); and Niall Ferguson, *The War of the World: Twentieth-Century Conflict and the Descent of the West* (New York: Penguin, 2006). Valuable essay collections include Clive Emsley, Arthur Marwick, and Wendy Simpson, eds., *War, Peace and Social Change in Twentieth-Century Europe*, 2nd ed. (Milton Keynes, UK: Open University Press, 2001); Roger Chickering and Stig Förster, eds., *Great War, Total War: Combat and Mobilization on the Western Front, 1914–1918* (Cambridge: Cambridge University Press, 2000); Roger Chickering and Stig Förster, eds., *The Shadows of Total War: Europe, East Asia, and the United States, 1919–1939* (Cambridge: Cambridge University Press, 2003); and Roger Chickering, Stig Förster, and Bernd Greiner, eds., *A World at Total War: Global Conflict and the Politics of Destruction, 1937–1945* (Cambridge: Cambridge University Press, 2005).

For civilian experiences during the First World War, see Tammy Proctor, *Civilians in a World at War, 1914–1918* (New York: New York University Press, 2010); Neil M. Heyman, *Daily Life during World War I* (Westport, CT: Greenwood Press, 2002); and Gail Braybon, ed., *Evidence, History, and the Great War* (New York: Berghahn Books, 2003). On the interwar years and the coming of the Second World War, see P.M.H. Bell, *The Origins of the Second World War in Europe*, 2nd ed. (London: Longman, 1997); Richard Overy with Andrew Wheatcroft, *The Road to Total War*, 3rd ed. (London: Vintage, 2009); and Martin Baumeister and Stephanie Schüler-Springorum, eds., *"If You Tolerate This …": The Spanish Civil War in the Age of Total War* (Frankfurt: Campus Verlag, 2008). Richard Overy, *The Morbid Age: Britain Between the Wars* (London: Allen Lane, 2009) is illuminating on fears of war in Britain.

Note

1 Quoted in Richard Overy, *The Morbid Age: Britain Between the Wars* (London: Allen Lane, 2009), 315.

1 | The Strains of Mobilization

Over the course of the 1930s, growing international strife led both politicians and many ordinary citizens to fear a terrible conflict was in the offing. But when the Second World War did actually begin, at different times for different countries, the demands it made upon ordinary life still constituted a shock for many. While the modes and timing of national mobilizations varied greatly, all states made increasing demands upon their populations. Economies were reoriented towards wartime production, and legislation was passed to direct the flow of labour. Countries made preparations for civil defence, and in some instances massive evacuations had to be carried out. Propaganda machines were put into effect, their capacity to reach large audiences enhanced by growing literacy and new technologies. Populations were called upon to unite in support of the national effort; enemies were harshly criticized and often demonized.

Wherever they lived, civilians experienced the pressures of war. For millions there was the constant concern about the fate of loved ones, whether they were serving in the armed forces or had become prisoners of war (POWs) or refugees. Those who relocated for war work faced many challenges, while those forced to evacuate had their lives thrown into upheaval. Rationing made for a more equitable existence, but there were always shortages and inconveniences. Black markets—illegal trade in violation of official rationing—were widespread. The impact of propaganda and the social changes taking place were alarming to many. People wondered about the implications of having friendly foreign troops stationed in their country and worried that outsiders might be spies. The greater mobility and independence of women was worrisome to some, and there was a sense that young people were out of control. Resentments that the burdens of war were not being equally imposed on different groups were easily sparked. During the war years class resentments, ethnic tensions, and social frictions of various kinds were all too evident.

Beyond these generalizations there were, of course, great national variations. Democracies such as Canada and the United States, remote from the battlefield, had a vastly different experience of mobilization from that of the Soviet Union, a totalitarian political system confronted with invasion. This chapter surveys those diverse experiences of mobilization. It focuses upon the major combatants who sustained a continuous war effort. It considers them roughly in the order in which they entered the conflict, outlining the general features of their mobilizations and assessing popular responses to those measures. The focus is primarily upon patterns of work and everyday life and the shifting popular mood until the later years of the war. The fate of civilians under foreign occupation—those who experienced the horrors of battle and persecution, as well as the final stages of the conflict—is considered in the succeeding chapters.

Japan and China

Though the Second World War is often dated as running from 1939 to 1945, there are good reasons for beginning with earlier developments in East Asia. As we have seen, Japan embarked upon an expansionist course with the invasion of Manchuria in September 1931. The ultra-nationalist Japanese government encouraged its people to see the conquest as an effort to modernize and civilize a backward land. Following a clash between opposing troops in July 1937, Japanese forces launched a full-scale offensive against China. The imperial government characterized this act of aggression as a major step in Japan's mission of leading Asia away from Western domination. It also launched a "spiritual mobilization" campaign, calling upon its people to forgo extravagances in support of the war effort. This was quickly accompanied by more concrete measures; in March 1938 a law was passed to expand the role of the state in the economy, giving it, among other things, the power to conscript labour. Business interests were directed towards producing for the war effort, with the Toyota Company, which had originally focused on cotton production, now making motor vehicles.

While Japanese forces conquered vast amounts of territory the Chinese continued to resist, and the campaign proved more difficult than originally anticipated. Economic restrictions in Japan began to bite; by 1939–40 rice shortages were reported in some districts. By then the imperial government was seeking to improve health and welfare provisions, for instance by passing a health insurance law as early as 1938, but it continued to gird the country for war by extending its mobilization efforts and further restricting the expression of opinion. In 1940 it celebrated the 2,600th anniversary of the creation of the Japanese empire and established the "Imperial Rule Assistance Association" to coordinate the country's various political parties in support of the war effort. As censorship of the press, radio, and film intensified, the government embarked upon a process of shifting school curricula to reduce Western influences and expand the role of physical education, with an eye towards preparing male children for military service. Women's and youth associations were created at the national level to instill patriotic values, and the government also sought to use community councils to promote its message. By the time of the attack on Pearl Harbor on 7 December 1941, the Japanese state had already gone a long way in terms of psychological and political mobilization. While it would be misleading to overstate the similarities between Imperial Japan and its Fascist and Nazi allies—traditional institutions remained much stronger, and a true one-party state had not been instituted—the demands being made upon its people were considerable.

How did the people respond? By and large, Japanese civilians obeyed, though there were hesitations and voices of dissent. Life had certainly become glummer. Strictures against extravagance extended to closures of dance halls in October 1940. As consumer goods were sacrificed in support of the war effort everyday life became more threadbare. One former schoolgirl recalled having to go without a coat all winter; her teacher suggested this hardship made for bodily discipline and served to remind the students of the sacrifices made by troops fighting in northern China.[1] This teacher, it would seem, was among the elements of Japanese society who embraced the official line. Not everyone was so enthusiastic. The relatively liberal *Women's Review*, for instance, avoided the growing criticism of Britain and the United States that was increasingly prevalent in the Japanese press. However, it adopted a less political line than it had before the war, and even this was unable to save it from eventually being shut down; some of its readers apparently objected to its outlook, which is suggestive of how sectors of opinion had become more xenophobic during the war. Richard

Storry, who later became an esteemed historian of modern Japan but in 1938 was a professor of English at a Japanese commercial college, captured the tensions between dissent and conformity. He observed that while some students criticized the attack on China and Japan's turn towards "fascism," powerful sectors of opinion—conservative politicians, the military, and many industrialists—supported the war, and much of the public felt duty-bound to support the government, even though many disliked its policy. Struck by the level of police surveillance, which he believed was widely resented, Storry nevertheless was sure that his students would fight and die for the Emperor.[2]

The situation worsened after Japan attacked the United States and the British Empire in December 1941. Despite early spectacular successes, which brought a range of new territories with vast natural resources under their control, after the Battle of Midway in June 1942 the war began to turn against the Japanese. While the government sought to obscure the extent of the defeats, it could not hide the growing privation on the home front, which resulted from meeting the needs of the military and an American submarine offensive against Japanese merchant shipping, which was exacting a heavy toll by 1944–45. Toshiko Marks, who had been a child in wartime Japan, recalled that by 1943 food shortages had become a serious problem, with people resorting to the black market in order to provide for their basic needs.[3] Children were often used to carry such goods, as they tended to be more successful in avoiding bureaucratic controls. While food distribution systems remained in place and civilians avoided starvation, malnutrition was prevalent. By 1944 the population had experienced a 17 per cent drop in their average daily calorie consumption since the start of the war; in comparison their British counterparts had suffered a 2 per cent drop.

Sustaining wartime mobilization thus became increasingly difficult. The Japanese government conscripted 1.5 million men for factory work; they were eventually joined by some 1.8 million students. But its deference to traditional values was such that the regime hesitated to direct women into factories, though it did pass a decree mobilizing single females in 1944. Still, women's participation in the workforce only rose by 10 per cent over the war, compared to 50 per cent in the United States. All of these urban workers faced long days—an average of 11 hours by 1944—as well as falling real wages, the result of tax increases and mounting inflation. Conditions in the countryside were little better, with women, the elderly, students, and white collar workers, including some business executives, stepping in to take the place of those sent to the front. Disaffection was particularly evident in the factories, where absenteeism, strikes, and work stoppages increased. One police report characterized the outlook of conscripted workers as follows: "From our miniscule incomes, food and clothing expenses are deducted; we get no pay as soldiers do for sickness or death.... There are such punishments as the guardhouse and wage cuts. It really makes you feel as though you're in jail."[4] But this bitterness did not translate into organized opposition. The extent to which ordinary Japanese people endured can be seen by the fact that economic output remained fairly steady until the final stages of the war.

China proved less successful in sustaining national cohesion during the war. To some extent this is not surprising, as the country had been in upheaval for decades. The Chinese empire had been overturned by revolution in 1911, and in the years that followed the country experienced social dislocation and political fragmentation, with much authority accruing to regional warlords. Since 1925 the Guomindang (GMD—Nationalist) movement, dominated by Jiang Jieshi, had begun to re-establish a central state, but it faced many obstacles. Warlords sought to preserve their influence, while the Chinese Communist Party (CCP) was emerging as an important rival. For a time in the 1920s the GMD and CCP were allies, but Jiang turned on the Communists in 1927, savagely repressing them. He persisted on this course even after the Japanese conquest of Manchuria. Indeed, Jiang had initially hoped to reach an agreement with the Japanese, whereby he would accept their conquests on the condition that Tokyo advance no further. But he found them un-cooperative, and nationalist pressure from elements of his own population to resist the invader proved overwhelming. Indeed, in December 1936 Jiang was kidnapped by a warlord—the former ruler of Manchuria—who insisted that he forge an alliance with the CCP against the Japanese. Jiang complied; an agreement was in the works when the Japanese began their general offensive against China in July 1937.

In the months that followed Chinese troops fiercely resisted the Japanese invaders. They inflicted significant casualties but were forced to retreat, surrendering key cities such as Beijing, Shanghai, and Nanjing; military and civilian casualties were very high. By late 1938 the fighting had stalemated. Jiang moved his capital to Chongqing, in a more remote southwestern region that was less economically developed than the populous coastal areas occupied by the Japanese.

The impact of the invasion was devastating. Hundreds of thousands of civilians—eventually millions—were killed by Japanese troops and aerial bombardment. Some 800,000 people drowned in floods after Chinese troops destroyed several dykes of the Yellow River in June 1938 in an attempt to slow the invaders' advance by flooding their path. Many more Chinese civilians became refugees. While precise figures are hard to come by, tens of millions fled their homes over the course of the war, some of them to neighbouring villages for short periods of time, others for years, moving deep into the southern and western provinces. Chongqing and other cities had to cope with an influx of newcomers, and tensions with the local population flared. There were inspiring cases of adaptation; students and faculty from universities all over China, for instance, came together to establish the Southwest United University in the city of Kunming. But daily life was trying for refugees and, indeed, for most ordinary people in what was now known as "Free China." The British journalist Freda Utley captured the plight of a group who arrived in the city of Wuhan in the spring of 1938:

> Old men and women and young mothers sat upon straw mats with babies and young children, thin, sad, hopeless in their misery, and many of them sick. I questioned one young woman who lay, very ill, upon a mat with a tiny baby beside her.... "Where is your husband?"
> "He has joined the guerrillas...."
> "Are you all alone, or have you a family here?"
> "Alone, my family has been killed."
> "How old is your child?"
> "Two weeks old; he was born on the road and I managed to walk on and get as far as this."[5]

Despite the immense suffering and dislocation, the regime held on. Jiang calculated that the Japanese offensive would eventually peter out and that the United States would be drawn into the war. In many respects he was proven correct, and eventually his regime achieved international recognition as an ally in the struggle against the Axis, with the United States in particular providing aid and advice. In return Jiang's government could point to significant contributions and sacrifices. Approximately 1 million Japanese troops were tied down in China, as Jiang refused to come to terms with the Japanese despite repeated entreaties (though GMD officials had held exploratory talks in 1940). But while Jiang stressed that he remained committed to the war against Japan, other priorities resurfaced, in particular the struggle against the Communists. By late 1939 cooperation between the two sides was breaking down, and armed clashes took place in 1940–41. Jiang seemed to be holding his best troops in reserve for a final showdown with the CCP, resulting in a more limited war effort against Japan.

This stance angered Jiang's allies and alienated significant elements of the population under his control. The situation was exacerbated by GMD governing policies; while the regime faced immense challenges, at least some of its citizens' growing discontent might have been avoided. Politically, Jiang attempted to mobilize opinion in support of the war effort, but the authoritarian character of his regime sharpened. He sought to concentrate power in his own hands, censored dissenting views, and relied increasingly upon a fearsome police apparatus under the infamous Dai Li. The economic situation also deteriorated precipitously. Government attempts to meet costs partly by printing more money encouraged serious inflation, while efforts to institute price controls failed. The regime's new southwestern base lacked infrastructure; though efforts had been made to relocate factories, only a relatively small number had actually been moved, and production was never able to meet needs. The government resorted to increasingly unpopular measures, notably a land tax, collected in kind, beginning in 1941. The implications of this move proved disastrous in the province of Henan, where the 1942 wheat harvest was decimated by drought. Officials still insisted upon collecting the tax in full, and in 1942–43 there was a famine in which 2 to 3 million people perished.

Civilians under GMD rule were becoming increasingly demoralized. While many privations were unavoidable, there was a perception that the regime was venal as well as repressive. Inflation and shortages compelled people to resort to the black market, and this encouraged a perception—with some basis in reality—that unscrupulous people, including individuals associated with the government, were profiting from the war. One 1944 newspaper editorial, never published because of censorship, described the situation in the following terms: "With the nation in hardship and the people in poverty, a small corrupt element is growing increasingly richer and living even more luxuriously. This rotten phenomenon, together with many other reactionary political factors, has lowered both the people's and the soldiers' morale nearly to the vanishing point."[6]

The GMD regime's deterioration was revealed in the spring of 1944, when Japanese forces launched the Ichigo Offensive, aimed at capturing US airbases in Nationalist China. Jiang's troops did not resist as fiercely as they had in the past; desertions were a serious problem. The lines stabilized not because of Chinese resistance, but because Japanese objectives were limited. Most strikingly, in Henan province farmers who had survived the famine displayed their hatred of the regime by attacking retreating soldiers, some of whom were buried alive. There were even plans by disaffected regional warlords and other political formations to overthrow Jiang. Though these ultimately amounted to nothing, they illustrated the extent to which the GMD regime had been gravely weakened over the course of the war.

Germany and Italy

In 1939–40 the war spread to Europe. Nazi Germany embarked upon its savage invasion of Poland on 1 September 1939, and then conquered much of Northern and Western Europe—Denmark, Norway, the Netherlands, Belgium, and France—in the spring and summer of 1940. On 10 June 1940 the Italian Fascist dictator Benito Mussolini, anxious for easy territorial gains in the wake of Nazi victories, took his country into the war on Germany's side. Both countries would ultimately go down to defeat, but Hitler's Reich, which enjoyed greater resources, military capacity, and popular support, proved more durable than its Italian ally.

Nazi Germany initiated the war in order to carry out an expansionist foreign policy, conquer an empire, and reshape Europe according to its racist ideology. However, the Third Reich's preparations for war were also conditioned by Hitler's determination not to repeat the experience of deteriorating civilian morale during the First World War. This meant that while rearmament was pursued with increasing intensity during the 1930s, to the point where labour and material shortages were becoming a problem by 1939, the regime avoided cutting off all consumer spending or warning the German public that protracted sacrifices might soon be required. The intention was that much of the burden would be borne by the subject peoples of Germany's new empire. An early sign of this came after the takeover of the Czech lands in 1938–39. While German officials were initially able to recruit thousands of Czechs to work voluntarily in Germany, as early as June 1939 Hermann Goering forecast that hundreds of thousands more would have to be coerced to do so to fulfill the needs of the Reich. These policies of aggressive expansion and exploitation were promoted by an increasingly powerful propaganda apparatus under the leadership of Joseph Goebbels. Since 1933 the media, subjected to tightening controls, had cultivated hostility towards the Western democracies and impressed upon the German people the need for unity, discipline, and combating internal threats, whether they be political or racial. The impact of this propaganda was likely amplified by the fact that Germany's rearmament had been accompanied by economic recovery and the near-elimination of unemployment by 1939, for it meant that Hitler began the war with significant, if not universal, reserves of popular support.

The Nazi regime still limited its demands on the German people in the early stages of the war. While its armed forces ravaged Poland in 1939 and prepared to move west in 1940, at home the Reich tread carefully in terms of wage controls and the regimentation of labour, after early attempts at a more rigorous policy were met with absenteeism and declining productivity. One important limitation on mobilization was the hesitation to conscript female labour. While it is true that large numbers of German women already worked outside the home, Hitler preferred that they focus on marriage and motherhood, which meant that in the early stages of fighting the Reich did little to direct more of them into war industry. That many soldiers' wives, though not those married to farmers or small businessmen, received substantial allowances while their husbands served, acted as a further disincentive. Throughout this period, the Nazis increasingly relied upon state-organized theft to provide for the German people. During the 1930s, property confiscated from the Jewish community had been auctioned off. As Germany expanded its European empire, vast resources, both in terms of goods and labour, became available. The Nazis strove to provide Germans with goods from the occupied territories at a favourable rate, mitigating the impact of ongoing rationing and controls.

In the early stages of the war public opinion on the home front shifted from initial caution to growing confidence. Though many Germans had approved of Hitler's foreign policy triumphs during the 1930s—which had been achieved without going to war—the mood was quiet following the attack on Poland. Returning from a visit to Berlin, a Swedish journalist observed that "Germany as a whole favours a short and victorious war—cheap, as far as biological losses are concerned—[rather] than a long and expensive adventure."[7] After six years in power the Nazi regime did have substantial support, but Hitler himself was more popular than the party in general, many of whose local officials were regarded as self-serving bullies. There were potential sources of friction: the rural population had benefited less from National Socialism than town and city dwellers, and some German youths expressed rebellion through embracing swing music or even brawling with the Hitler Youth. Nevertheless, the *Wehrmacht*'s victory over Poland in 1939 and especially its triumph over France in 1940 were extremely popular. The reaction of Lore Walb, a 21-year-old history student at the University of Munich, to France's surrender illustrates how Hitler's personal reputation benefited: "It's only now that we can truly estimate our Leader's greatness. He has proved his genius as a statesman but his genius is no less as a military commander ... with this Leader, the war cannot end for us in anything except victory! Everyone's firmly convinced of it."[8]

In the weeks and months that followed, many Germans found the inability to subdue Britain unnerving. Moreover, while there was a widespread acceptance of propaganda claims that the invasion of the Soviet Union in June 1941 was a justified pre-emptive strike against a bloodthirsty and revolutionary Bolshevik enemy, failure to defeat that enemy soon became an even greater source of concern. Then, on 11 December 1941, Hitler declared war on the United States; though the Nazi leader scorned what he saw as a degenerate population, many German elites, and much of the public, feared its economic power and military potential. The scope of the conflict was widening, and civilians in the Third Reich could not be isolated from the consequences of accepting Hitler's policies. After the victories in 1939–40 soldiers had sent packages home consisting of goods "liberated" from Germany's new empire, but in the winter of 1941–42 a special drive had to be launched to acquire winter clothing for the troops stalled outside of Moscow. By the following spring, fleets of British bombers were attacking German cities, soon joined by American forces. In 1942 Axis forces suffered major reverses in North Africa. They were defeated in the Battle of El Alamein in October and were then unable to stop Allied landings in North Africa in November. Germany's worst defeat to that point soon followed. The battered remnants of the Sixth Army surrendered to the Soviets at Stalingrad on 2 February 1943, after the failure of a five-month effort to take the city.

It was impossible for the Nazi regime to hide the scale of the Stalingrad defeat. Over the course of the battle 200,000 troops had been killed, and over 200,000 captured. Goebbels responded by trying to galvanize opinion in support of a "total war" effort, giving an energetic performance before a (selected) audience in Berlin soon after the defeat, where he ended with the peroration "Arise, storm, and break loose!" At this time a series of measures were taken to intensify German mobilization. Rations had already been reduced, to popular displeasure, at earlier stages in the war, and while they would never reach the starvation levels of the First World War people now complained that adequate food was increasingly hard to come by. The government also tried to decree the shutting down of non-essential businesses, though public discontent soon blunted that initiative. The Reich also began to register women for labour conscription, though it still moved cautiously in that regard. Caution was not evident in the ongoing exploitation of foreign labour. By 1944 the number of foreign workers in Germany reached a total of some 7 million. Some came voluntarily and worked under conditions not so different from that of their German counterparts. But millions, the majority of them from occupied Eastern Europe, were essentially slave labourers.

How did German civilians respond to the demands for greater sacrifice? There were growing signs of dissent and disaffection. Domestic surveillance revealed that from 1943 onwards respect for the Nazi Party and even Hitler himself, whose public appearances were fewer and fewer, was in decline. Some civilians flouted key tenets of the regime. For example, significant numbers of German women engaged in romances with foreign workers, even though the government had enacted many restrictions involving harsh punishments for this, especially in the case of East Europeans. Yet while public enthusiasm waned, Hitler was correct in his boast that the implosion of German civilian morale that had taken place in 1918 would not be repeated. The Nazis' previous successes, and their efforts at indoctrination, had created a core of committed supporters.

Moreover, the majority of Germans who were not hard-core Nazis had become bound to the regime in a variety of ways. Many had benefited from its policies, including its efforts at imperialist plunder. Nor could they step out of line easily. Denunciation by one's neighbours, co-workers, or even family members was a possibility, and the Reich punished domestic opponents with mounting severity. Allied bombing campaigns encouraged hatred and determination to carry on. The government's shrill propaganda campaign about what awaited Germans should the Red Army invade also convinced many that it was necessary to support the war effort. Visiting a Berlin restaurant, two Swiss journalists recorded the views of one group of patrons, consisting not only of military officers but also scientists and engineers. These individuals were critical of the regime's mistakes, but they could see no alternative to continuing on: "What is it that will happen to us when the Russians march in? Better to lose everything than to back down now.... The terrible sacrifices of our soldiers should not be in vain. We have to win!"[9] The fact that the unsuccessful attempt on Hitler's life, made on 20 July 1944, was followed by widespread expressions of public disapproval, including pro-government rallies in major cities, suggests that the Third Reich enjoyed significant support into the closing months of the war.

In comparison, Fascist Italy entered the war less well-prepared than Germany and soon found its mobilization effort in trouble. Mussolini had exhausted his armed forces through repeated campaigns during the 1930s and believed that when Italy entered the war in June 1940 it would soon be over. His government did little to modify the tax structure to ease financing of the war; the ration scheme only covered part of the population's requirements. By 1941 Italy was directing only 23 per cent of its gross domestic product to the war effort, compared to over 50 per cent in Britain, and over 60 per cent in the case of its German ally. Publicly, Mussolini implored his people to "rush to arms and show your courage, your tenacity, your valour!" Yet scant months before, he had privately denigrated them as a "race of sheep," doubting whether they could ever be forged into a virile nation.[10] Soon after declaring war the Italian armed forces began to experience what proved to be a long string of humiliating defeats; the success of German armies offset these setbacks at first but also reduced Mussolini's image in the eyes of his own people.

Initially, there was some Italian support for the war. The Fascist trade unionist Tulio Ciannetti claimed that "almost the totality of us Italians in a few days [in May-June 1940] were engulfed by admiration and enthusiasm for the astonishing German victories."[11] This claim was exaggerated, but official surveillance pointed to a degree of acceptance, fed by expectations of relatively little sacrifice. Yet public engagement was not robust—before long, declining living conditions and military failures combined to degrade morale. The meagreness of official rations necessitated resorting to the black market and bartering, but not all Italians could afford to do so, and by 1942 hunger was becoming a significant problem in some areas, affecting productivity and morale. One Milan clerk noted how "in our office, there's a general feebleness around; several hours before closing work is practically suspended. The men smoke furiously."[12] Allied bombing also took a considerable toll, killing 64,000 people. Various social fissures appeared as the war dragged on. Italy's substantial peasant population often tried to hoard food for the challenges they rightly suspected lay ahead, causing friction with urban dwellers. Regional animosities rose to the surface; some Milanese reportedly expressed satisfaction that Rome had to share in the misery of being bombed in 1943. In general, people focused upon their private lives and concerns, to the detriment of the Fascist war effort.

As Italian forces suffered defeats in the Balkans and North Africa, and as the United States joined the war—an event that aroused much concern, given perceptions of US power and personal family ties between the two countries—support not just for the war but willingness to tolerate the government itself evaporated. Membership in the Fascist Party rose in the early years of the war, but by 1942 thousands were refusing to renew. The alliance with Germany grew increasingly unpopular. As Mussolini's government directed agricultural exports, and growing numbers of workers, to the Reich, accusations arose that Germans were being fed at Italians' expense. The police, who tried to keep close tabs on public opinion, noted dissent even from unexpected quarters. Maria Ciocca, a baker's wife from Vinovo (near Turin), had a son in the army and a husband who kept his opinions to himself. She did not: the authorities noted with concern how she now "denigrated the Axis powers and persuaded the ignorant in her town that the war would be lost."[13]

In 1943 matters came to a head. Afflicted with shortages and confronted with further defeats—including the capture of thousands of troops in Tunisia—protests became more numerous. In March 1943 a series of strikes began in the factories of Turin and soon spread to Milan and elsewhere. While Italy's underground Communist movement played a role in sparking these, they took on a popular character, with as many as 100,000 workers involved. Though many of their demands were concrete, centring on wages and conditions, the political nature of their discontent with Fascism was clear. Ultimately Allied invasion, combined with the decision of King Victor Emmanuel III with support from elements of the political elite to dismiss and arrest Mussolini on 25 July 1943, ended Fascist Italy's war. But for many Italians the worst was yet to come, as additional German troops swarmed into the country much faster than the new government of Marshal Pietro Badoglio anticipated. The final two years of war would see the country turned into a battleground, with foreign armies and rival political formations engaged in bloody conflict.

Britain, the Commonwealth, and the Empire

The British experience of mobilization during the war proved to be quite different. While those on the home front experienced privation and suffering, and often expressed discontent, the country proved capable of sustaining a massive war effort. During the opening months of the conflict—the era of the "Phoney War," when British and French troops engaged in little action against the Germans—the steps taken by the government were relatively cautious, but even then the populace found their lives disrupted. Fears of German bombardment led to the imposition of "the blackout" and the evacuation of thousands from large urban centres to the countryside. One British industrialist found the people he hosted "fundamentally clean and decent" but noted that many other residents of the village where he lived "have found their evacuees, whether children or mothers or both, very hard to bear."[14] Children in particular might be stung by harsh treatment from insensitive or resentful hosts. But others, such as the future novelist Eva Figes, found their new lives to be a great adventure. Though sometimes hungry, she recalled how "I revelled in my new-found sense of independence, finding things out, being a person, riding a bike as though I had grown wings."[15]

Following the stunning victories of the German army in Western Europe in the spring of 1940—which drove British forces off the continent—a sense of crisis mounted. The public cheered the evacuation of over 100,000 servicemen from Dunkirk, but soon German bombers began striking British cities. An invasion was widely anticipated; thousands of men ineligible for military service entered the Home Guard, and civilians also participated as Air Raid Wardens. Although the authorities reported evidence of panic and defeatist sentiments, there was also a widespread sense of defiance. Winston Churchill, who had assumed office as prime minister in May 1940, reinforced this mood. The impact of the air raids will be discussed more fully in Chapter 3, but it must be noted here that the period from the summer of 1940 to the spring of 1941 was characterized by a complex psychological mixture of fear, exhilaration, boredom, and frustration deriving from the constant threat of attack, the long periods of waiting in shelters, and the disruptions to everyday life. While people applauded the successes of the Royal Air Force (RAF) and the fears of invasion later receded, the night raids of the Luftwaffe stretched nerves to the limit, as the British people realized that a long and difficult road lay ahead.

Churchill's coalition government deepened mobilization. Minister of Labour Ernest Bevin directed workers to sectors where they were deemed vital—such as coal mining—and forbade them from leaving establishments where they were defined as essential. Strikes were outlawed. Beginning in 1941 women between the ages of 18 and 60 were registered for war work, as well as men over the age of 41. The system of rationing was refined, and citizens were encouraged to plant gardens. Subsidized "British restaurants" were established to provide another option, especially for workers with higher caloric requirements. In all, citizens of this liberal democracy found their lives increasingly regulated, leading the Canadian diplomat Charles Ritchie to observe that "Living in London is like being an inmate of a reformatory school. Everywhere you turn you run into some regulation designed for your protection."[16] But the government recognized that people had limits and made concessions. It strove to ensure that supplies of tobacco and beer were available, though the latter was watered down.

Home Secretary Herbert Morrison rejected demands to ban horse racing on the grounds that access to public entertainment was good for morale.

Though there was plenty of grumbling and social friction, the collective response of the British people was energetic. Britain mobilized its people more fully than its US ally or its German enemy; by 1944 one-third of the entire population was in civilian war work, along with another 22 per cent in the armed services. The number of women in paid employment expanded from nearly 5.1 million in 1939 to 7.75 million by 1943. Some housewives who could have been exempted from war work because of family obligations took jobs anyway, motivated by patriotic duty but also need, for the allowances paid to soldiers' wives were less generous than in Germany. Those women who did not take up paid employment often still engaged in support of the war effort in any number of ways, including volunteer work. Some, such as Nella Last, a 50-year-old housewife who devoted spare time to the Women's Volunteer Service, believed the war had transformed the fabric of their domestic lives. As early as March 1940 she commented that "I always used to worry and flutter round" when her husband grew moody, "but now I just say calmly, 'Really dear, you *should* try and act as if you were a grown man and not a child of ten, and if you want to be awkward, I shall go out—ALONE!'"[17]

The economic strains were huge. By 1941 the British government had run out of money and was reliant on Lend-Lease Aid from the United States. By late 1943 there were critical shortages of personnel. Had the British people also reached their limit? Certainly there were strains. When a German invasion seemed imminent labour disputes had been rare, but as the danger lessened and the pressures of war work accumulated, strikes rose alarmingly by 1944 in spite of the legal ban. Notwithstanding official emphasis on the need for social solidarity, class tensions persisted; workers were accused of being coddled, while the middle and upper classes were derided for using their wealth to subvert rationing and other restrictions. Social resentment could be vented upon "outsiders." Despite widespread disapproval of Nazi persecution, for instance, Jews were sometimes accused of being "un-British" because they were supposedly fixated upon self-preservation and material gain. "Foreigners" were also the target of suspicion—even if they were allies in uniform. Britain hosted millions of foreign troops over the course of the war, with especially large US and Canadian contingents. Though they were generally welcomed by the British people, there was conflict over issues such as actual and perceived rowdiness as well as competition for female attention. US soldiers were resented by some British civilians for their high pay and attentiveness to local women. As one expression went, the GIs were "overfed, oversexed, and over here."

The war was widely regarded as detrimental to public morals and personal relationships. Crime rates rose; violations of blackout and rationing regulations partially account for this trend, but there were also increased incidents of robbery and brothel-keeping. Commentators observed that lack of parental supervision, typically the result of longer workdays and other war-related commitments, made for undisciplined youth. In particular, there was anxiety about teenage and young women "running wild," their desire for sexual adventure heightened by the presence of foreign troops. There was particular racially motivated concern about relationships between British women and African-American servicemen. Officials from both countries tried to limit contact, with some success. Marriages also ran into trouble. The prospect of lengthy separation encouraged many couples to marry sooner rather than later, but once they were apart there could be temptation for one or the other partner to stray. For servicemen there was a widespread belief that this was unavoidable, and it was something that could be easily concealed if the person was stationed far from home. A woman who "drifted," on the other hand, was more likely to attract harsh criticism. The personal consequences could be very difficult. In cities such as Birmingham officials reported an increase in the number of "irregularly conceived" children born to married women. Higher divorce rates were another result of the war.

But various trends and policies helped to sustain British morale. Rationing made for monotonous diets, and there was always the temptation of the black market, but historians tend to agree that the system achieved its essential goal of providing adequate nutrition to the population. Indeed, those who had lived below the poverty line in the 1930s found they ate better during the war. The scourge of unemployment was almost eliminated, and thanks to price controls real wages eventually increased. Though there were few consumer goods to be had, at least legally, the government's flexibility regarding the availability of tobacco, spirits, and entertainment meant that there were opportunities to "take time off from the war." In contrast to their German counterparts, Britons gradually had reason to be more optimistic. The entry of the Soviet Union and the United States into the war as allies, and the gradual improvement in military fortunes that took place following victories such as El Alamein (1942) and Stalingrad (1943) tended to buoy spirits, though sometimes people became overly optimistic that the war would soon end and were disappointed when it did not. And while giving rise to some discord, the presence of Allied troops in Britain itself could be comforting.

As the war entered its final stages British civilians were tired. Impatient for victory and the return of their loved ones, many also hoped that their years of wartime sacrifices would be acknowledged. The evolution of the public mood can be seen in the enthusiastic reception of the Beveridge Report, which appeared in December 1942. Written by an academic turned civil servant, the report called for the rationalization and improvement of social insurance benefits, a national health care system, a child allowance, and a general effort to reduce unemployment. This government publication sold more than 100,000 copies within a month of its appearance, and opinion polls suggested widespread approval. Hopes for a better future were accompanied by cynical remarks that Beveridge-style reforms would never be implemented, yet this could not hide the fact that the report voiced and reinforced a conviction that the hardships of the 1930s, and the efforts of the British people since 1939, merited large-scale social reform.

Especially during the dark months between the French surrender in 1940 and before the Soviet Union and United States entered the war in 1941, British propaganda depicted the country as a besieged island standing alone. Though this was a striking way to galvanize the population, it must be remembered that it was the entire British Empire that went to war. Except for the Irish Free State, civilians in the self-governing dominions of Australia, Canada, New Zealand, and South Africa mobilized against the Axis. Though propaganda emphasized the extent to which they were engaged in a common effort, and for many individuals there was a real sense of solidarity with "the mother country," the character of mobilization varied according to the particular circumstances. Canada made a major contribution to the Allied war effort, both militarily and in terms of economic output. The government introduced rationing and price controls, though it did not regulate the labour force to the same extent that Britain did. Both Australia and New Zealand supported Britain with troops and material, but after Japan entered the war the Australians in particular shifted focus. The Japanese launched a number of air raids on the country; one attack, on the northern city of Darwin in February 1942, killed 243 people. Amidst growing concerns about an invasion, the government began extending controls over the workforce, tightening ration restrictions, and raising taxes. By comparison, South Africa's effort was more restrained, largely because many Afrikaners opposed intervention in the conflict, with some ultra-nationalists harbouring sympathy for Germany. The country made an important economic and voluntary military contribution, but it did not conscript troops.

All of the Dominions experienced economic expansion, with attendant social changes and frictions. In Canada the unemployment that had plagued the country during most of the 1930s evaporated; millions of people found new jobs, often moving to do so, and cities such as the port of Halifax experienced serious housing shortages. In Australia and New Zealand, as well as other British possessions such as Newfoundland and Bermuda, local populations adjusted to the presence of US troops. As in Britain, they were often welcomed enthusiastically. Estelle Rolfe, who volunteered at the American Service Club in Wellington, New Zealand, recalled that "They had tons of money and they used to give flowers and chocolates and cigarettes and everything."[18] This was appreciated by many—youths as well as women—though as in Britain it could also lead to antagonism. In all of these states there was an appreciable, if sometimes short-lived, expansion in the employment of women; in South Africa black participation in the urban workforce also grew appreciably. The latter process did not, however, lead towards more equitable race relations. Though restrictions that had prevented Africans from living in urban areas were relaxed in 1942, and the country's Deputy Prime Minister, J.H. Hofmeyr, indicated that he hoped the colour bar would one day be no more, African hopes for further change went unrealized. Nevertheless, the economic changes that did occur encouraged the development of an African working class that continued to press for better conditions.

There were ethnic problems in the other Dominions as well. After Pearl Harbor fears of Japanese encroachment intensified long-standing prejudice on Canada's West Coast, which led to the "evacuation" of nearly 21,000 Japanese-Canadians inland, many of whom had their property expropriated. In the province of Quebec a significant current of Francophone opinion was opposed to the idea of conscripting young men to fight overseas in a "British" war, to the point where there were protests in Montreal. The Aboriginal peoples of Canada, Australia, and New Zealand all participated extensively in wartime mobilization, both militarily and as civilian labourers. This could mean better jobs for a time, but it did not bring an end to the general inferiority of their economic circumstances or their second-class civic status. In Canada, First Nations people volunteered for the military in high numbers, but they did not achieve equal voting rights until 1960. Australian Aborigines gained better access to social benefits during the war, but their standard of living remained lower than that of whites, and they did not attain full citizenship status until 1967. New Zealand Maori were somewhat better served in terms of political rights; a small number of seats in the country's parliament were reserved for them. They were also experiencing rapid social change, as wartime opportunities led to growing migration to cities such as Auckland. But many Maori had trouble finding decent housing and were cut off from traditional community support. Maori elders worried about the impact on their traditions.

As the prospect of victory neared many people within the Dominions, while anxious about loved ones and grating under restrictions, were proud of their involvement and hopeful about the future. In some ways akin to their US neighbours, many Canadians were experiencing increased prosperity. Real though the divisions in the country were, commitment to the war effort had considerable depth; in the city of Verdun, Quebec, which had substantial English- and French-speaking populations, there were communal frictions but also a clear, shared commitment to defeating the Axis. In Australia there was resentment about British inability to ward off Japanese encroachments, but morale held. Even in South Africa, where the war effort remained more controversial, over half of the white men who enlisted in the armed forces were of Afrikaner descent; some 42,000 Africans also signed up, though they were generally restricted to non-combatant roles.

In contrast to the largely independent if often parallel mobilization policies pursued by the Dominions, civilians in Britain's colonial territories had little say in the direction of the war effort, a state of affairs that many resented. In India constant nationalist pressure had led the British to concede a degree of internal self-government during the 1930s, but in 1939 the British viceroy declared war on Germany without consulting Indian politicians; he was constitutionally empowered to do so, though his approach was highly resented. With a population of over 300 million, India was prized as a source of military and civilian manpower, materials such as textiles and clothing, and a growing amount of military ordnance. After the Japanese attacked and conquered British possessions in Asia in 1941–42—notably Hong Kong, Singapore, Malaya, and neighbouring Burma—India was threatened with invasion. Defence preparations intensified, and the country hosted hundreds of thousands of British, US, and Chinese troops; its industrial base expanded, and vast quantities of new roads, air fields, and hospitals were built. But Indians also experienced higher taxes and shortages. The availability of key staples such as rice was reduced, and there were serious problems with food distribution.

In 1943 disaster struck in the territory of Bengal. There were massive harvest failures, for which neither the central government nor local authorities were well-prepared. The British Raj proved unable to implement sufficient coordination with other Indian provinces that had food surpluses. In peacetime, British authorities might have been able to alleviate the problem with rice from East Africa, but huge shipping losses to German U-Boats in 1942 made transport far more difficult. Beyond that, the hesitation of Churchill's government to divert supplies intended for military and other civilian needs—a hesitation strongly criticized by British Viceroy Field Marshal George Wavell—meant that sufficient relief was slow in coming. Famine ravaged Bengal for months; as many as 3 million people may have starved to death.

The Bengal Famine further weakened British prestige in India, at a time when it was already waning. Most leading Indian nationalists, notably Mohandas Gandhi and Jawaharlal Nehru, detested Nazism and militarism, but they still sought independence and deeply resented the newly strengthened demands of the British. The leading political movement, the Indian National Congress, had protested India's abrupt entry into the war by ceasing to serve in government bodies. The British tried to stabilize the situation, and their wartime control, with promises of a new constitution and even complete independence after the conflict ended. But the negotiations failed, and in 1942 the Congress launched a campaign calling on the British to "Quit India." The imperial state responded swiftly, arresting and imprisoning thousands. Protests continued at the local level, however, and 50 battalions were deployed to maintain control. India continued to support the war effort economically and militarily, but there was widespread discontent with the British. The latter were determined to hang on during the war and worked with the Congress's rivals, notably the Muslim League, to facilitate control, but it seemed increasingly clear that the days of the Raj were numbered.

The British also found the Mediterranean, a region they deemed of fundamental importance to their future global power status, increasingly difficult to manage. In the opening months of the conflict there had been hope that the region would be relatively calm, but Italy's entry into the war changed that, and as German troops were sent in to bolster Mussolini's failing efforts the situation seemed even more menacing. The inhabitants of the tiny island of Malta, which provided Britain with an excellent base for harassing Axis shipping lanes, lived in a state of siege, under constant aerial bombardment until 1943. Mediterranean cities such as the Egyptian port of Alexandria and the Trans-Jordanian capital of Amman also came under attack. The British reinforced their already significant presence in the region with troops and labour brigades from throughout the empire, sparking construction and manufacturing projects that often involved local civilians. In Palestine local industry focused on producing basic military supplies, and farmers were given loans and encouraged to expand production to meet military needs. In Egypt wartime circumstances prevented the export of the country's vital cotton crop in 1940 and 1941, so the British intervened to buy it up in order to avert economic disaster. Legislation was passed requiring a partial shift to food production, but even then there were serious food shortages, predictably accompanied by rationing and an expanding black market.

The British presence in Egypt aroused considerable political controversy. Egypt was an independent state rather than a colony, but it had been occupied by Britain since 1882, and by treaty it was compelled to support Britain's war effort. This did not go down well with many Egyptians, and in fact there was considerable pro-Axis sentiment in the country. The capital city of Cairo, which also hosted Britain's Middle Eastern Command, was a hotbed of espionage during the war; during a period of severe shortage in January 1942 rioters stormed bakeries in the city, and there were also demonstrations in support of the German commander Erwin Rommel, whose troops, some hoped, would soon arrive. The British had already compelled Egypt's King Farouk to dismiss one prime minister in 1940, and in February 1942 they surrounded the royal palace with tanks and ordered the king to appoint a pro-British government or abdicate. Farouk gave way to British demands, but Egyptian nationalists would not soon forget what they regarded as an intolerable humiliation.

In neighbouring Palestine, a British mandate, the situation was also tense. During the 1920s and especially the 1930s there was growing friction between Palestine's expanding Jewish community and the local Arab majority. With British approval, Zionist organizations—who wanted to establish a Jewish state in the Holy Land—promoted Jewish migration and land purchases. Elements of the Arab community feared that they would eventually be marginalized and became increasingly hostile to Jewish settlement, while the British engaged in an uneasy balancing act between the two sides. In 1936, the British quelled an Arab revolt only with difficulty. In 1939 Britain tried to mollify the Arabs by sharply restricting Jewish immigration—at a time when Jews were fleeing anti-Semitic persecution in Europe. This shift in British policy upset much of the *Yishuv* (Palestinian Jewry), but given that Britain was fighting Nazi Germany, the community still gave strong support to the imperial war effort. Some 27,000 Palestinian Jews served in the British armed forces, while about 63 per cent of the Jewish workforce was eventually engaged in war production. Palestinian Arabs were far more ambivalent, though not completely receptive to the pro-Nazi propaganda of Hajj Amin al-Husseini, the former Mufti of Jerusalem now exiled in Berlin. As the threat of Axis invasion receded, and resentments intensified with respect to British refusals to admit more Jewish refugees when European Jews were being murdered on a massive scale, elements of the *Yishuv*, hoping to establish an independent Jewish state, turned against the British. For some this led to terrorist activities; Britain's Resident Minister in the Middle East, Lord Moyne, was assassinated by a member of the radical Zionist Lehi movement in 1944.

In Britain's sub-Saharan African colonies the situation was less explosive, but the demands of war still provoked unrest. These territories were remote from British military campaigns against Italian forces in East Africa during 1940–41, but their manpower was seen as a valuable resource, as were their raw materials. This was the case especially after the Japanese conquests of 1941–42 deprived the British of some Asian colonies and reduced the availability of rubber and tin, which was now sought in West Africa. As in India, throughout the war the colonial state grew more intrusive, with significant consequences. British officials directed local headmen and chiefs to conscript men for the armed forces, and in some instances also for civilian war work such as road construction, the expansion of military facilities, and even work on private, white-owned plantations, though some British officials balked at going this far. The construction of bases and the development of port facilities meant that cities such as Mombasa in Kenya experienced rapid growth; its African population expanded from 55,000 to 100,000 during the war years. Throughout these colonies propaganda emphasized that Africans must participate in the defence of their lands from a German enemy who would reduce them to the status of slaves.

All of these processes were highly disruptive. Greater economic output was accompanied by shortages of consumer goods and price inflation, making life more difficult for urban and rural populations alike. Towns and cities swelled with people looking for steady work, but it was not always to be found. Conscription caused havoc in many communities, as local elites were often resented for their complicity in separating families, and many individuals sought to evade the authorities. Yet in the end, the African contribution to the war effort was far more substantial than many British officials thought it would be in 1939; it should be noted that while there was plenty of coercion the majority of civilian labour was voluntary. Children from a village in eastern Nigeria illustrated how efforts to rouse support for the war could affect the lives and behaviour of people who at first blush seemed very distant from the conflict. The colonial Nigerian government sought to encourage palm kernel production with a "Crack for Victory" campaign (as each nut had to be cracked open); the children responded by creating a "cracking song," in which a feared local species of lizard, nick-named "Hitler," was to be cracked on the head to help win the war.[19]

Some Africans tried to win greater compensation for their efforts; dock-workers and railwaymen sought to unionize and thus attain better pay and conditions. In the process they did not hesitate to draw attention to the gap between reality and the British propaganda that insisted that the war was being fought for democracy. A letter written to their employers in 1943 by a group of dockworkers in Dar es Salaam (Tanganyika) provides an example of this sentiment: "from day to day we are being kicked and beaten just not like human beings ... we are being told that we are at war with the Nazi German because the Nazis want to enslave the world, how is it that an English is making us a slave in the face of the capital of this country?"[20] Thus in Africa as well as India and the Mediterranean, Britain's all-out effort required and received the support of millions in the empire, but it also exposed and enhanced the grievances of colonial populations.

The Soviet Union and the United States

The last two great powers to join the war against the Axis were the Soviet Union, following the German invasion on 22 June 1941, and the United States, after the Japanese attack on Pearl Harbor on 7 December 1941. Both countries made decisive contributions to the Allied victory. Central to their achievements was the production of enormous quantities of armaments, itself the result of intense mobilization. However, it would be hard to imagine sharper contrasts between civilian experiences in the two soon-to-be superpowers. For the population of the Soviet Union the years between 1941 and 1945 were ones of horrifying loss and punishing sacrifice. Some 25 million people, 16 million of whom were civilians, lost their lives. In the United States the war was the catalyst for an economic boom that, though accompanied by significant social problems, also saw rising living standards and new opportunities for millions of people.

The Soviet people had already endured Stalin's policies of crash industrialization, collectivization, and terror, but now they faced an even greater test. The country's military had already been quite active; the Red Army had clashed with Japanese forces in 1938–39; cooperated with the Germans in partitioning Poland; and conducted a major, very costly campaign against Finland in 1939–40. But inept leadership and early Axis successes in 1939–40, which left Europe dominated by Germany, created a situation in which the Soviets would have to fight the Nazis under the most desperate of circumstances. Although tensions were on the rise between the two dictatorships in 1941, Stalin was committed to his strategy of cooperation with Hitler to the point that he refused to believe repeated warnings of an impending attack, leaving his forces in vulnerable forward positions. This meant that the German-led invasion force of 3 million men initially achieved great success, capturing vast amounts of territory and inflicting huge losses. By December, when the offensive was finally halted outside of Moscow, 2.6 million Soviet soldiers had been killed and 3.3 million taken prisoner. Most of the western Soviet Union, which accounted for 40 per cent of the country's grain output, two-thirds of its coal, pig-iron, and aluminum capacity, and approximately one-third of its industrial workforce, was now under enemy occupation, with these resources at the disposal of the Nazis.

In the years that followed millions of Soviet citizens perished as a result of being trapped in besieged cities, such as Leningrad and Stalingrad, or as victims of a murderous German occupation. Life in the unoccupied Soviet Union, away from the front lines, was difficult enough. Stalin's regime struggled to respond; its efforts were characterized by a high degree of state planning but also considerable improvisation. Civilians were drafted in the thousands to build defensive fortifications around Moscow and elsewhere; in the opening months of the war hundreds of thousands were also enrolled in armed militia units, which sustained very heavy casualties, leading to restrictions upon their use from 1942 onwards. As in China, evacuation of factories took place, but on a larger scale, consummate with the higher level of industrialization. Over 2,500 major enterprises, and as many as 50,000 smaller workshops, were relocated east of the Ural Mountains beyond the range of German bombers. Evacuated workers had to reassemble the factories, sometimes on open ground in winter conditions. The British journalist Alexander Werth observed that "people worked because they knew it was absolutely necessary—they worked twelve, thirteen, sometimes fourteen or fifteen hours a day; they 'lived on their nerves'; they knew that never was their work more urgently needed than now."[21]

The Soviet workforce was already tightly regulated, but the regime now required mandatory labour service in addition to regular work. Moreover, infraction of workplace rules could lead to imprisonment; leaving one's job without permission meant the possibility of five to eight years in prison. The huge rural population of the Soviet Union was squeezed very hard. Most agricultural work was carried out on state-organized collective farms by women, youths, and the elderly, often in very primitive conditions as equipment and livestock were needed for military use. The infamous Soviet forced labour camp system, commonly known by the acronym GULAG (Main Camp Administration), had taken in millions of prisoners during the 1930s, and they now became an important source of labour for the war effort. The entire population was affected by rationing quotas, which varied widely based on one's job. Those who did not work, or who were not a dependant of someone who worked, were not entitled to rations. Though the urban population did gain access to small land allotments to grow food, shortages were a critical problem, especially in the early years of the war, and Soviet citizens sometimes had to survive by eating nettles, grass, and acorns.

The shock of invasion and scale of early defeats initially weakened the iron grip of Stalin's regime on ordinary citizens. In some territories the Germans were initially regarded as liberators from Communist rule, and the Third Reich found collaborators from various elements of the population in the occupied areas. Even in the territories that remained under Stalin's control, dissent was also palpable. The Moscow police reported one female factory worker commenting the day after the invasion that "It's good that the war has begun. Life in the USSR has become unbearable. Forced labour and hunger bother everyone, there should be an end to all this."[22] The authorities noted a belief in some quarters that German occupation would only fall hard on Communists and Jews, leaving "ordinary people" alone. Indeed, expressions of anti-Semitic sentiment, such as accusations that Jews were avoiding military and labour service, grew more prevalent in the early stages of the war. In October 1941 the capital of Moscow witnessed widespread panic in response to word of approaching German troops; reports of looting and disorder led to the declaration of a state of siege.

Stalin's regime employed a mixture of techniques to maintain control and motivate wills. Repression was extensive. Expressions of defeatism and dissent resulted in prison sentences. Entire nationalities suspected of actual or potential disloyalty—such as the ethnic Germans of the Volga region, the Crimean Tatars, and the Chechens, as well as thousands of people from the recently annexed Baltic republics—were ruthlessly deported to Central Asia or Siberia; some 3 million people may have been affected, thousands of whom perished. Yet the Soviet government also recognized the need to consider the evolving popular mood and to loosen some restrictions. Though they told the population virtually nothing about the huge casualties being sustained, for a time newspapers such as *Pravda* concentrated less on promoting the tenets of Marxism-Leninism and more on the experiences and motivations of ordinary people, who emphasized not only their love for their families and homeland but also their ferocious hatred of the enemy. Restrictions on religious institutions, particularly the Russian Orthodox Church, were loosened to serve spiritual needs and to nourish patriotic sentiment. Simple but powerful appeals to defend the motherland against the foreign invader were effective. Many Soviet citizens supported their government's efforts but also saw themselves as fighting a people's war. Ben Levich, a Jewish scientist, recalled that, "It was our country we were defending, our war effort."[23]

As the war turned against Hitler, Soviet civilians grew more confident. The victories of the Red Army at Stalingrad in the winter of 1942–43, and at the Battle of Kursk the following July, raised hopes for victory. Lend-Lease Aid from the United States provided critical support, especially in items like trucks, locomotives, and aviation fuel. The achievements of Soviet workers were also prodigious; despite enormous losses of territory and resources, they still out-produced the Germans in artillery, tanks, and aircraft. But living conditions remained straitened, and people were aware that the sacrifices were not being borne equally: party members often had greater access to food. Moreover, with victory in sight the regime began to tighten its grip again. For example, while stories about Stalin in the Soviet press had receded in the early stages of the war, as the military situation improved his role as supreme warlord was enhanced; letters were published thanking him for the liberation of individual cities from Nazi rule. Soviet citizens experienced many changes as a result of the war, but appreciably greater political freedom would not be one of them.

Like the Soviet Union, the United States came into the war as a result of a surprise attack. The Japanese raid on Pearl Harbor of 7 December 1941, which aimed at crippling the US Pacific Fleet, killed over 2,400 civilians and military personnel. But the parallels between the two countries quickly end. The mainland United States was largely spared the ravages of war, though there were two instances of shelling and some balloon-borne bombs on the Pacific coast and German submarine attacks off the Atlantic coast.

But in the early months of war fear of further Japanese strikes, exacerbated by reports of early American and Allied defeats in the Pacific and Southeast Asia, triggered fear and hatred. The day after the attack on Pearl Harbor, 16-year-old Frank Keegan of Santa Rosa, California, drove with five friends to nearby Bodega Bay, where they waited behind dunes with a rifle and two shotguns for a Japanese attack.[24] It never came, but in the months that followed suspicion of and animosity towards Japanese-American communities along the Pacific coast heightened. During the spring and summer of 1942 roughly 112,000 Japanese Americans were interned in isolated, austere detention camps, where most remained until the later stages of the war. The fact that neither the German nor Italian-American communities were treated in this way highlights the significance, though not the uniqueness, of ethnic and racial divisions in US society.

In December 1941 the United States was not well-prepared to fight a global war. The country's navy was sizeable, but its army was only the sixteenth-largest in the world, and many of its military aircraft were obsolete. Despite the reforms of President Franklin Delano Roosevelt's New Deal, unemployment had remained stubbornly high since the Great Depression; in 1940 it was still near 15 per cent. Yet the US economy had tremendous potential, and it shifted to military production at an impressive rate, with the last civilian automobiles rolling off the plant lines in Detroit in February 1942. Historians have noted that the organization of the US war effort was haphazard; Roosevelt created a series of agencies for this purpose, but many had limited or overlapping mandates. It was not until 1943 that the Office of War Mobilization, which supervised all other agencies directing mobilization, was established. Furthermore, the role of private business was influential. Many prominent executives provided advice or ran agencies on a voluntary basis—they were known as "Dollar-a-Year Men," as a nominal salary was mandated by law. It should also be noted that while the role of the state expanded greatly, compared to other combatant nations there were limits to how far Washington would go in terms of directing the population. For instance, the US Congress would not approve a bill to draft female workers, despite favourable public opinion on this issue.

Nevertheless, within a relatively short period of time the United States was playing the role of "arsenal of democracy" that Roosevelt had promised it would. By the end of 1942 it was already out-producing the three leading Axis states *combined* in terms of aircraft, warships, tanks, and artillery. By 1944 it accounted for some 40 per cent of all weapons made around the globe; by 1945 US industrial production had doubled in a four-year period.

Millions of people experienced life-altering changes as a result. Aside from the significant proportion of the population that entered military service (over 10 per cent), some 15 million people changed residence, many of them to take up positions in war industries. In geographic terms there were marked population shifts; 8 million people moved between states, primarily to the North and West from the South and East. The states of Washington, Oregon, and especially California embarked on a period of frenzied growth. Some 2 million African Americans left the South during these years, many of them moving to cities in the North and West. Some 6.5 million women entered the workforce for the first time, eventually constituting over one-third of workers. Between 1940 and 1942 unemployment was largely eliminated and shortages had appeared in some sectors.

As with all the major combatants, the US government emphasized the need for social harmony, especially when it came to ensuring production. Shortly after Pearl Harbor Roosevelt brought together business and labour leaders to conclude an agreement that stressed the need for the peaceful resolution of industrial disputes; a commitment was made to avoid strikes and lock-outs for the duration of the war, and a National War Labor Board was created to resolve disputes. At first the results were impressive, with the level of strikes plummeting. But there were limits to this restraint. Roosevelt had sought to cap incomes at $25,000 as a sign of his commitment to restrict profiteering and to convince workers that sacrifices would be borne by all levels of society. But opposition to the measure in Congress, which cited the effectiveness of the profit motive, proved too strong and it was defeated. Before long, elements of the US working class were expressing discontent with harsh conditions and inadequate compensation. The situation was especially difficult for coal miners. In contrast to some other groups, their real incomes were falling because of inflation, and the conditions they faced were extremely hazardous; hundreds were injured every week. In 1943 they went on strike, seeking significant wage increases; the leader of the United Mine Workers (UMW), John L. Lewis, was accused of sabotaging the war effort and aiding the Axis. The government took control of the pits, but eventually UMW won major concessions. By the end of 1943 railroad and steelworkers were on strike; by 1944 the level of walkouts was even higher.

Clearly, while new opportunities for work were available, life could be difficult. For the millions of people on the move, decent accommodation was in many cases harder to find, and locals were not always welcoming towards newcomers. In wartime Seattle shipyard workers were sometimes forced to sleep in their cars. At the enormous bomber factory constructed at

Willow Run, Michigan, local residents resisted the building of new housing and the expansion of the local school system, despite the obvious growing need. Families came under strain, often because one parent was in the military and the other in war work, with benefits for military wives proving inadequate. One employee with the Office of Civil Defence in California reported that "I have seen children locked in cars in parking lots in [the San Fernando] valley and I have seen children chained to trailers in San Diego."[25] As in other countries, the excitement and danger of wartime tended to encourage marriage but also facilitated conditions for divorce. Reports of juvenile delinquency rose; the weakening of family bonds and the existence of job opportunities for many youth created circumstances in which they had greater freedom—which sometimes had detrimental social consequences.

Though the level of state intervention was less than in many other countries, the US government did make demands on its people. Rationing was introduced for gasoline, sugar, coffee, butter, meat, and canned goods. Other consumer goods, such as clothing, were not officially rationed, but the demands of the military meant that quantity and variety soon declined. The government also launched seven war bond drives, imploring people to do their patriotic duty. One particularly striking advertisement depicted a woman working a drill press with the following caption: "Her husband in a Jap prison camp in the Philippines ... her father in a Formosa prison camp ... she leaves 4 children at home ... while she works 8 hours a day—but she invests 25% in War Bonds. Do you think you're buying enough?"[26] The advertisement was crafted by the manufacturers of Pepsodent toothpaste, highlighting the importance of commercial advertisers in shaping wartime US propaganda. The message promoted by the state-run Office of War Information, established in June 1942, was initially intended to be restrained and factual in tone. But as writers from private ad firms were drafted to these organizations, more populist messages—which also tended to predominate in private advertising, radio, and film—came to the fore. During a visit to the United States in 1942, British historian Denis Brogan recalled receiving a butter pat during a commercial flight; its label read "REMEMBER PEARL HARBOR."[27]

From the start Americans displayed deep commitment to the war effort. The first nationwide drive to buy war bonds brought in $39 million dollars in a single day, while the seventh and final one raised $26.3 billion—almost twice what the organizers had hoped for. Civic organizations both old and new were extensively involved in a variety of ways. The American Women's

Voluntary Service, founded in 1940, eventually enrolled some 350,000 members, including supporters from the Chinese, Mexican, and African-American communities. Initially the organization aimed to provide support in the event of aerial bombardments. When these did not occur, it took on tasks such as selling war bonds and delivering food to remote military posts. Scrap metal drives provided a way for local communities to get involved, and many did so with enthusiasm. A state-wide 1942 drive in Nebraska, sponsored by the Omaha *World-Herald*, amassed a total of 135 million tons of scrap, 103 pounds for each person in the state. Children often played a prominent role in these initiatives. A nation-wide campaign held in October 1942 resulted in an estimated 30 million children bringing in 1.5 million tons of scrap metal, according to the War Production Board. Publicity for these activities could take on a belligerent tone. The children's magazine *Jack and Jill* recounted the story of four brothers who formed a club as part of a local drive, proclaiming "We're after scrap to get a Jap."[28]

The story was not solely one of sacrifice, however. Given the increased pressures of wartime as well as official restrictions on many consumer goods, Americans spent more on going to the movies, buying magazines, and other forms of entertainment—for many, memories of deprivation during the 1930s encouraged these impulses even more. Advertisers catered to these sentiments and also raised expectations for a prosperous postwar future. An advertisement for Nash Kelvinator refrigerators featured a woman wishing for the return of her spouse, declaring "I know you'll come back to me.... Everything will be here, just as you left it"—along with a new refrigerator.[29] Seeking distractions and hopes for a better tomorrow were to be expected, but more than a few individuals flouted the law. Gasoline rationing led to the production of counterfeit coupons by organized crime, which accounted for as much as 5 per cent of the gas sold nationwide. A writer for *Woman's Home Companion* visited eight cities in 1943 and was shocked at the level of black market activity. During her trip she had been able to buy 90 pounds of food and consumer goods, all without spending ration points; the items included a pair of nylon stockings sold by a bank president who kept a supply in his bottom desk drawer. Even the bond drives had their limits; large investors accounted for nearly three-quarters of bond purchases, though the majority of the US population did buy at least one bond.

There were also ethnic tensions. Propaganda emphasized how the diversity of the US population was a great asset and contrasted it to the emphasis on racial purity by enemies such as the Third Reich. Soon after Pearl Harbor Roosevelt called upon Americans to avoid falling into the trap of ethnic prejudice, but this injunction was not always followed, even by his administration. The internment of Japanese Americans remained in effect until the end of 1944. Anti-Semitic sentiments intensified in wartime America. Jews were blamed by some for getting the country into the war and were accused of shirking military service and engaging in profiteering; in fact, one 1944 poll found that Jews were considered to be a greater threat than German or Japanese Americans. African Americans continued to experience discrimination, enduring segregation and frequent marginalization in the armed forces. On the home front, the wartime boom created new employment opportunities, allowing many to leave, for example, domestic service. One woman observed that "Hitler was the one that got us out of the white folks' kitchen."[30] Moreover, when confronted with the threat of a march on Washington from black leaders in 1941, President Roosevelt issued an executive order banning employment discrimination in government or defence industries.

But segregation was entrenched in the South and ostracism was widespread in the North; in the summer of 1943 Detroit, which had experienced rapid growth because of wartime production, exploded into rioting. There had already been incidents such as strikes by whites protesting the promotion of black workers, but in June a fistfight between a white man and a black man turned into a full-scale clash; 25 blacks and nine whites were killed, hundreds were injured, and 1,800 people were arrested. That same summer Mexican and African-American youths fought with servicemen, civilians, and police in riots that began in Los Angeles but soon spread to other cities. Many of the youths were "zoot-suiters"; their elaborate clothing was identified with rebellious, even criminal behaviour. That white servicemen often started the fighting was overlooked.

The realities of civilian life in wartime in the United States were thus more complex, and more conflict-ridden, than those who today extol the achievements of "the greatest generation" might like to think. Yet millions of Americans did what was asked of them, and often more. People certainly made sacrifices, even though these were often in the form of accepting limits on gains rather than the sheer deprivation suffered by so many civilians in Europe and Asia. In the final stages of the conflict many looked forward to even greater prosperity and the return of stable home life. And while the strains of mobilization had revealed the salience of prejudice, not all groups experienced it to the same degree. For example, the large Italian-American community, some 5 million people, had long been treated as second-class citizens. But in spite of the fact that some members displayed support for

Mussolini, the fact that Italy was not seen as a major threat, as well as the electoral importance of this group, meant that the government soon removed the designation of "enemy alien" from the 600,000 Italians who were not yet citizens and took steps to facilitate their naturalization. Such measures have led some historians to conclude that the war was an important step in the integration of Italian Americans on more egalitarian terms. For other groups, such as African Americans, the road ahead was less clear, but living standards improved and the desire for change was strengthened. As Walter White, head of the National Association for the Advancement of Colored People, wrote in 1945, "World War II has immeasurably magnified the Negro's awareness of the disparity between the American profession and practice of democracy."[31]

Conclusion

The civilian experiences of mobilization defy easy generalizations. Nevertheless, it is striking to note the extent to which most populations bore the demands made upon them by their governments, not always in good cheer but often with great fortitude. The reasons for this varied; repression figured more prominently in the cases of Germany and the Soviet Union than they did with the democracies, though in both countries there was also substantial popular support for the war effort, nurtured by years of propaganda as well as fear of what the enemy would do. In other states a faltering of the popular will was more obvious. In Fascist Italy military defeats and privations led to growing alienation from the regime. In Nationalist China the devastation wrought by the Japanese forces and the shortcomings of Jiang's government eventually sapped once considerable reserves of patriotism and sacrifice. But even in these cases the populace did not overthrow the government. Mussolini was dismissed from office, and his successors attempted to change sides; a reduced Nationalist China held on until the Japanese surrender. For countries such as Britain, the United States, and the Soviet Union popular commitment was re-energized by the knowledge that things were getting better over the course of the war. But in Nazi Germany and Imperial Japan, despite the clearly turning tide, public willingness to endure remained intact to a significant degree. While the consensus in support of these regimes frayed as the war went on, both were defeated militarily, not by a collapse of civilian morale.

While most people managed as best they could, they were also transformed by their wartime experience. Millions had their lives shattered by loss of loved ones and livelihoods; austerity could lead to lasting physical and psychological problems. At the same time, many people found camaraderie, love, adventure, and a sense of purpose. While there was an overwhelming desire to resume a stable life, for a host of groups the war raised hopes for longer term change. This complex legacy would shape the post-1945 world for decades.

Further Reading

Joanna Bourke, *The Second World War: A People's History* (Oxford: Oxford University Press, 2001), is a stimulating overview. Gordon Wright, *The Ordeal of Total War* (New York: Harper and Row, 1968) and Alan Milward's *War, Economy, and Society 1939–1945* (Berkeley, CA: University of California Press, 1977) are classics. I.C.B. Dear and M.R.D. Foot, eds., *The Oxford Companion to World War II* (Oxford: Oxford University Press, 2001) and David Kennedy *et al.*, eds., *The Library of Congress World War II Companion* (New York: Simon and Schuster, 2007) are key reference works. Valuable essay collections include Jeremy Noakes, ed., *The Civilian in War: The Home Front in Europe, Japan, and the USA in World War II* (Exeter, UK: University of Exeter Press, 1992); David Reynolds, Warren Kimball, and A.O. Chubarian, eds., *Allies at War: The Soviet, American, and British Experience, 1939–1945* (New York: St. Martin's Press, 1994); John Bourne, Peter Liddle, and Ian Whitehead, eds., *The Great World War 1914–1945*, Vol. 2: *The Peoples' Experience* (London: Harper Collins, 2000); and Gordon Martel, ed., *The World War Two Reader* (New York: Routledge, 2004). Two volumes edited by Richard Aldrich provide a wealth of contemporary civilian and military accounts: *Witness to War: Diaries of the Second World War in Europe and the Middle East* (London: Doubleday, 2004) and *The Faraway War: Personal Diaries of the Second World War in Asia and the Pacific* (London: Doubleday, 2005). See also Studs Terkel, *"The Good War": An Oral History of World War Two* (New York: Pantheon Books, 1984).

For Japan, see Thomas Havens, *Valley of Darkness: The Japanese People and World War Two* (New York: W.W. Norton, 1978); for China, Lyman Van Slyke provides a clear overview in "Nationalist China, 1937–1945," in Lloyd Eastman *et al.*, eds., *The Nationalist Era in China 1927–1949* (Cambridge: Cambridge University Press, 1991); see also Lloyd Eastman, *Seeds of Destruction: Nationalist China in War and Revolution 1937–1949* (Stanford, CA: Stanford University Press, 1984), and Diana Lary and Stephen McKinnon, eds., *Scars of War: The Impact of Warfare on Modern China* (Vancouver, BC: University of British Columbia Press, 2001). Stephen MacKinnon, *Wuhan, 1938: War, Refugees, and the Making of Modern China* (Berkeley, CA: University of California Press, 2008) focuses on the early stages of the Sino-Japanese War.

Excellent works on Nazi Germany abound. Richard Bessel, *Nazism and War* (New York: Modern Library, 2004) is concise and lucid. More detailed accounts include Martin Kitchen, *Nazi Germany at War* (London: Longman, 1995) and

Richard Evans's *The Third Reich at War* (London: Penguin, 2008). For Italy, see Philip Morgan, *The Fall of Mussolini: Italy, the Italians, and the Second World War* (Oxford: Oxford University Press, 2007) and the relevant chapters of R.J.B. Bosworth, *Mussolini's Italy: Life under the Fascist Dictatorship, 1915–1945* (New York: Penguin, 2006). On Britain, Angus Calder's *The People's War: Britain 1939–1945* (London: Jonathan Cape, 1969) is a pioneering work; more recent contributions include Robert Mackay, *The Test of War: Inside Britain 1939–45* (London: UCL Press, 1999); Sonya Rose, *Which People's War? National Identity and Citizenship in Wartime Britain 1939–1945* (Oxford: Oxford University Press, 2003); and Juliet Gardiner, *Wartime Britain 1939–1945* (London: Headline Book Publishing, 2004).

Ashley Jackson, *The British Empire and the Second World War* (London: Hambledon Continuum, 2006) integrates discussion of the various home fronts with an account of military operations. For Canada, see Jeffrey Keshen, *Saints, Sinners, and Soldiers: Canada's Second World War* (Vancouver, BC: University of British Columbia Press, 2004) and Serge Durflinger, *Fighting from Home: The Second World War in Verdun, Quebec* (Vancouver, BC: University of British Columbia Press, 2006). For Australia, see Joan Beaumount, ed., *Australia's War, 1939–1945* (St. Leonard's, NSW: Allen & Unwin, 1996). Nancy Taylor, *The Home Front: The New Zealand People at War*, 2 vols. (Wellington, NZ: Historical Publications Branch, Department of Internal Affairs, 1986) provides a wealth of detail. On India, there is Johannes Voigt, *India in the Second World War* (New Delhi: Arnold-Heinemann, 1987). For Britain's African colonies, see David Killingray and Richard Rathbone, eds., *Africa and the Second World War* (New York: St. Martin's Press, 1986).

On the Soviet Union, Alexander Werth's *Russia at War 1941–1945* (New York: Carroll and Graf, 1964) is engrossing; more recent analyses include John Barber and Mark Harrison, *The Soviet Home Front, 1941–1945: A Social and Economic History of the USSR in World War II* (London: Longman, 1991); Robert Thurston and Bernd Bonwetsch, eds., *The People's War: Responses to World War II in the Soviet Union* (Urbana, IL: University of Illinois Press, 2000); and Rebecca Manley, *To the Tashkent Station: Evacuation and Survival in the Soviet Union at War* (Ithaca, NY: Cornell University Press, 2009). For the United States, see Kenneth Rose, *Myth and the Greatest Generation: A Social History of Americans in World War II* (New York: Routledge, 2008); earlier works include William O'Neill, *A Democracy at War: America's Fight at Home and Abroad in World War II* (New York: The Free Press, 1993); John Morton Blum, *V was for Victory: Politics and American Culture During World War II* (New York: Harcourt Brace Jovanovich, 1976); and Richard Polenberg, *War and Society: The United States 1941–1945* (Philadelphia, PA: Lippincott, 1972).

Notes

1 Thomas Havens, *Valley of Darkness: The Japanese People and World War Two* (New York: W.W. Norton, 1978), 10.

2 Ian Nish, "Japan," in Jeremy Noakes, ed., *The Civilian in War: The Home Front in Europe, Japan and the USA in World War II* (Exeter, UK: University of Exeter Press, 1992), 94–95.

3 Nish, "Japan," 97–98.

4 Quoted in Havens, *Valley of Darkness*, 95–96.

5 Quoted in Stephen Mackinnon, *Wuhan, 1938: War, Refugees, and the Making of Modern China* (Berkeley, CA: University of California Press, 2008), 49–50.

6 Quoted in Lyman Van Slyke, "Nationalist China, 1937–1945," in Lloyd Eastman *et al.*, eds., *The Nationalist Era in China 1927–1949* (Cambridge: Cambridge University Press, 1991), 169.

7 Axel Heyst, 4 December 1939, quoted in Richard Aldrich, ed., *Witness to War: Diaries of the Second World War in Europe and the Middle East* (London: Doubleday, 2004), 100.

8 Quoted in Richard Evans, *The Third Reich at War* (New York: Penguin Press, 2008), 135.

9 Quoted in Peter Fritzsche, *Life and Death in the Third Reich* (Cambridge, MA: Harvard University Press, 2008), 289.

10 Quoted in Anthony Cardoza, *Benito Mussolini: The First Fascist* (New York: Pearson Education, 2006), 146.

11 Quoted in Richard Bosworth, *Mussolini's Italy: Life under the Fascist Dictatorship, 1915–1945* (New York: Penguin, 2006), 457.

12 Quoted in Philip Morgan, *The Fall of Mussolini: Italy, the Italians, and the Second World War* (Oxford: Oxford University Press, 2007), 62.

13 Quoted in Bosworth, *Mussolini's Italy*, 479–80.

14 Sir Raymond Streat, 10 September 1939, quoted in Aldrich, ed., *Witness to War*, 71.

15 Quoted in Robert Mackay, *The Test of War: Inside Britain 1939–45* (London: UCL Press, 1999), 165.

16 Quoted in Mackay, *Test of War*, 172.

17 Nella Last, 14 March 1940, quoted in Aldrich, ed., *Witness to War*, 131.

18 Quoted in Christopher Pugsley, "New Zealand: 'From the Uttermost Ends of the Earth,'" in John Bourne, Peter Liddle, and Iain Whitehead, eds., *The Great World War 1914–1945*, Vol. 2: *The Peoples' Experience* (London: Harper Collins, 2000), 227.

19 Ashley Jackson, *The British Empire and the Second World War* (London: Hambledon Continuum, 2006), 224.

20 Quoted in Nicholas Westcott, "The Impact of the Second World War on Tanganyika, 1939–1949," in David Killingray and Richard Rathbone, eds., *Africa and the Second World War* (New York: St. Martin's Press, 1986), 155.

21 Alexander Werth, *Russia at War 1941–1945* (New York: Carroll and Graf, 1964), 218.

22 Quoted in Mikhail Gorinov, "Muscovites' Moods, 22 June 1941 to May 1942," in Robert Thurston and Bernd Bonwetsch, eds., *The People's War: Responses to World War II in the Soviet Union* (Urbana, IL: University of Illinois Press, 2000), 120–21.

23 Quoted in Rebecca Manley, *To the Tashkent Station: Evacuation and Survival in the Soviet Union at War* (Ithaca, NY: Cornell University Press, 2009), 196.

24 Charles Alexander, "The United States: The Good War?" in David Reynolds, Warren Kimball, and A.O. Chubarian, eds., *Allies at War: The Soviet, American, and British Experience, 1939–1945* (New York: St. Martin's Press, 1994), 285.

25 Quoted in Kenneth D. Rose, *Myth and the Greatest Generation: A Social History of Americans in World War II* (New York: Routledge, 2008), 111.

26 Quoted in Rose, *Myth and the Greatest Generation*, 118.

27 Quoted in John Morton Blum, *V was for Victory: Politics and American Culture during World War II* (New York: Harcourt Brace Jovanovich, 1976), 16.

28 Quoted in Robert Kirk, "Getting in the Scrap: The Mobilization of American Children in World War II," *Journal of Popular Culture* 29 (1995): 228.

29 Quoted in Blum, *V was for Victory*, 101.

30 Quoted in William O'Neill, *A Democracy at War: America's Fight at Home and Abroad in World War II* (New York: The Free Press, 1993), 245.

31 Quoted in Blum, *V was for Victory*, 219.

2 | Living under Occupation

Hundreds of millions of people experienced occupation during the war. All the major combatant states, including Britain, the United States, and above all the Soviet Union, took control of foreign lands. This chapter, however, will focus on the wartime empires established by the leading Axis states, Germany and Japan. At its height, the Third Reich asserted control over most of Europe, as well as a huge swathe of Soviet territory. The Japanese empire included vast Chinese territories, Korea, most of Southeast Asia, and numerous Pacific islands. Both empires were the product of frighteningly ambitious ideologies. They stressed the innate superiority of their own people and regarded those they subjugated as either simply a resource to be ruthlessly exploited or as obstacles to the creation of the empire who were to be eliminated. Millions perished as a result of these policies. In the end, both empires overextended themselves, underestimated their foes, and suffered total collapse.

Though the parallels are striking, there were differences between the German and Japanese empires. Nazi racism was more systematic than its Japanese counterpart. Despite their shared anti-Communism and hostility to liberal democracy, the Third Reich was not in a position to exploit anti-Western, anti-colonial sentiment in the way Japan was. Nonetheless, each caused profound disruptions in the daily lives of, as well as immense suffering for, the people over whom they ruled. Though some civilians were able to preserve a semblance of normal life, punitive rationing, forced labour, horrific punishments, summary executions, and wholesale genocide were the lot of millions of Europeans and Asians in these occupied territories.

While the majority of people living under occupation wanted nothing more than to survive and avoid trouble, few could avoid making choices about how to behave. Many accommodated to foreign rule in order to sustain daily life, while seeking to avoid enthusiastic cooperation. This was particularly the case early in the war, when it seemed unlikely that the occupiers would be defeated. Sometimes those who initially chose this course of action later decided that occupation was intolerable and engaged in resistance, which itself took on many forms, ranging from efforts to mobilize opinion to taking up arms. Resistance was very courageous and very dangerous, as it often invited reprisals against entire communities. At the other end of the spectrum, there were those who engaged in collaboration with the occupier in a variety of ways, whether out of commitment to a cause, personal attachments, or self-interest.

Occupation was thus often a profoundly divisive experience. Wartime circumstances could intensify old hatreds, while competition for scarce resources often pitted neighbours against one another. But occupation could also bring people together as they tried to sustain daily life and to preserve their spirits and dignity. Increasingly this quest for solidarity was expressed by the rise of resistance movements, which by war's end had galvanized millions of people—minorities in their own countries, but significant numbers nevertheless—into various forms of anti-regime activities. But not all resisters had the same goals. Some desired social revolution as well as liberation from the occupier, while others were as fearful about the rise of Communism as about ridding their country of Nazi or Japanese occupation. In Europe, the rise of resistance movements encouraged social and political radicalization and polarization. In Asia they were often accompanied by the strengthening of anti-colonial nationalism in the empires of Britain, France, and other West European states.

The Third Reich in Eastern Europe

As we have seen, Hitler's Germany began its quest for empire in Central Eastern Europe, annexing Austria in the spring of 1938 and taking the Sudetenland from Czechoslovakia at the end of September that year. In both cases, the Germans of these regions became citizens of the Reich, while the Jewish communities were persecuted and terrorized. The situation in Bohemia and Moravia, occupied in March 1939 and transformed into a protectorate under direct German rule, was different as it was the first time the Reich had taken direct control over a substantial non-German speaking population. Czechoslovakia's German minority was granted Reich citizenship but Czechs were not; Slovakia was reconstituted as a puppet state of the Reich. Thereafter, Germany expanded to the east by force of arms, subduing Poland in a brutal campaign in the autumn of 1939. As per the Nazi-Soviet Pact of 23 August 1939, eastern Poland was annexed by the Soviet Union. Germany annexed some of western Poland, while the remainder was transformed into the "General Government," a separate jurisdiction firmly under Nazi control.

Though he turned his attention north and west in the spring of 1940, expansion in the East was never far from Hitler's mind; by that summer he was already planning an invasion of the Soviet Union. In April 1941, both to shore up Fascist Italy's faltering campaign in Greece and to protect Germany's flank against potential trouble from the Kingdom of Yugoslavia, German forces conquered both countries. The Reich placed Greece under the control of a puppet government, and German soldiers shared occupation duties with Italian and Bulgarian troops. Yugoslavia ceased to exist; Germany and Italy annexed some of its territory, while Bulgaria occupied part of Macedonia. Serbia was reconstituted as a German satellite. In Croatia, the Axis created a puppet state, installing the ultra-nationalist Ustaša movement as the new government. Then, on 22 June 1941, the Third Reich launched its boldest attempt at expansion yet, invading the Soviet Union with 3 million troops, supported by some 600,000 Romanian, Hungarian, Finnish, Italian, Slovak, and Croat forces. Although they would never destroy Stalin's regime, the Germans conquered vast areas of Soviet territory. At the height of its territorial expansion in September 1942, the Reich ruled over some 70 million Soviet citizens.

Hitler and his colleagues had terrifying ambitions to decimate the inhabitants of Eastern Europe and open it up to German colonization. In the long term, the Nazis hoped that tens of millions of Europeans would be removed from their new territories through forced relocation, starvation, or murder. In the short term, the East was to be plundered for its resources and for its labour. The majority of the over 7 million foreigners brought to work in Germany during the war came from there; most of them had been coerced.

There was some variation in policy towards different groups, albeit within a general context of racist brutality. For the time being the Czechs were to focus upon producing for the Nazi war economy, but elements of their population were selected for Germanization, and the long-term Nazi goal was to fully "integrate" the Czech lands. As for the Poles, the Nazis quickly set to work eradicating their national identity. A million people were expelled from the Polish territories annexed by Germany to the General Government, which was primarily intended to be a reservoir of labour. The Nazis also conducted a systematic campaign of terror against Poland's educated classes. As Hitler put it on 2 October 1940, "There can be only one master for the Poles, and that should be the German ... therefore all representatives of the Polish intelligentsia are to be killed."[1] An estimated 48,000 people from the country's intellectual professions were murdered during the war, including 57 per cent of its lawyers and judges, and 29 per cent of its clergy. To ensure the continuing subjugation of the population, Polish education was banned in the annexed territories and forbidden beyond the secondary level in the General Government. As many as 200,000 "suitable" Polish children were abducted for potential "Germanization." The inhabitants of eastern Poland, occupied by the Red Army, also suffered intense repression, including the deportation of up to 1.5 million people into the Soviet interior; after the German invasion in 1941 those who remained behind experienced the horrors of Nazi rule.

The Balkan states were less central to Nazi plans for racial restructuring, and until 1943 the Germans shared occupation duties with their allies, above all Fascist Italy, which controlled Albania and had a presence in both Yugoslavia and Greece. Mussolini had his own policies for the "Re-Italianization" of strategic areas, and the benevolence of his armies must not be overstated. Although Italian troops engaged in hostage-taking and shot civilians, especially in Yugoslavia, the judgement that they were comparatively more restrained than their German counterparts has stood the test of time. Even so, the peoples of the region suffered immensely. In Greece, German food requisitions ignored local shortages and the impact of a British blockade, resulting in a famine that may have killed up to a quarter of a million people. In Yugoslavia, the satellite state of Croatia embarked upon its own program of mass murder (see Chapter 3). In Albania the Axis appealed to local nationalists by giving the country the Yugoslav province of Kosovo, where Albanians were the majority population.

There were potential German allies among various nationalities in the occupied Soviet Union. The Baltic States—Latvia, Lithuania, and Estonia—had only recently come under Soviet control; the brutal deportation and execution of thousands of their inhabitants had naturally aroused great hatred. Millions of Ukrainians, Belarusians, and Russians had suffered under Stalin's repression. To the south various groups, including Muslim

Crimean Tatars, Buddhist Kalmyks, and the legendary Cossacks, deeply resented Soviet repression of their traditional economic, cultural, and religious practices. Under these circumstances, it is not surprising that a substantial number of communities initially regarded the Germans as liberators. The occupiers took little advantage of this. While German officials promised to restore religious liberties, to eliminate collective agriculture, and to restore private farms, in practice they tended to retain the collective system for their own use. As for the restored religious institutions, they often became instruments of German control, with some clergy reporting on their congregations to the occupying forces.

Various military officers, civil servants, and even Nazi party officials wanted to go further in cultivating alliances with local populations, and in a few cases they made concessions. In much of the occupied Soviet lands the Germans shut down universities, but in the Baltic States they continued to operate. Some of the nationalities of the Caucasus were exempted from having to send workers to the Reich. However, the impulse for boundless exploitation, intensified by racist ideology, generally won out. Cities such as Kiev were deliberately starved in order to reduce the Slavic population. People who tried to evade being conscripted to work in the Reich could find their homes burned. Occupation forces sometimes held parents hostage until their children agreed to go work in Germany. An infamous remark by SS leader Heinrich Himmler encapsulates the dominant outlook of the Nazi leadership: "Whether 10,000 Russian women collapse with exhaustion in the construction of an anti-tank ditch for Germany only interests me insofar as the ditch gets dug for Germany."[2]

Predictably, the occupation exposed and intensified social divisions. The few concessions made by the Germans, such as the cancellation of debts owed to Jews by Polish peasants, were often intended to stir ethnic tensions. Nazi attempts to favour the German minorities of Eastern Europe—*Volksdeutche*—were not always successful but certainly had an impact. Traditional class structures often lost their meaning: members of the professions found themselves out of work, with no demand for their skills. It was those with practical skills, or those who were particularly cunning, determined, or lucky, who now tended to fare best.

Within these traumatized societies Nazi persecution of East European Jews quickened. During the invasion of Poland in 1939 German forces shot thousands; the invading troops also took pleasure in humiliating them, for instance, by pulling out the beards of Orthodox men. In the months that followed, Polish Jews were deported to ghettos in cities like Warsaw and Łódź. In these ghastly places they struggled to survive. Nazi officials debated whether they should simply starve or be exploited for their labour, but in practice deliberate overcrowding and shortages meant that malnutrition and disease did their grim work. By 1941 German inhabitants of the city of Warsaw averaged 2,613 calories a day in rations; Poles got 669 and Jews a mere 184. No one could survive on such an amount. If people lacked resources, they starved; if they had them, recourse to the black market or selling goods to the occupiers became necessary. Such activities also encouraged competition and thus divisions within ghetto communities.

The Nazis created a system in which Jews were intended to be complicit in their own subjugation and destruction, though they led Jewish leaders to believe productive communities might survive. "Jewish Councils," often consisting of prominent citizens, were established at German behest to administer the ghettos; the occupiers also created Jewish police forces to preserve order. Some of these authority figures were suspected of being corrupt and became highly unpopular, but the situation was complex. Council heads, such as Adam Czerniakow in Warsaw, desperately mediated between the needs of their people and the demands of the occupier. Czerniakow reached his limit when the Nazis began to deport Jews, including children, from the Warsaw ghetto to the Treblinka death camp in 1942. Unable to prevent or limit the deportations, he took his own life. Mordechai Rumkowski, head of the Łódź Jewish Council, governed in an authoritarian fashion and made very controversial decisions, enforcing a demand to deport the very young and the elderly from the ghetto in September 1942. It bears noting, however, that Nazi officials encouraged Rumkowski to think that if the ghetto's inhabitants were effective producers for the German war effort, at least some of them would survive. Indeed, some 60,000 Jews survived in Łódź until the summer of 1944, longer than any other ghetto, but in August the entire community, Rumkowski included, was sent to Auschwitz.

Faced with grim conditions and agonizing choices, many inhabitants of the ghettos nevertheless sought to foil German measures aimed at dehumanizing them by defying restrictions on children's education, the preservation of religious traditions, and the holding of cultural events. In the Kovno ghetto, a Mrs. Segal persisted in teaching Hebrew and Jewish traditions from the fall of 1941 until the spring of 1943, despite being prohibited from doing so.[3] Jewish social services tried to assist orphans and others in particular need, receiving some financial support from co-religionists outside occupied Europe. Jewish youth groups continued to operate, providing vital camaraderie. Cultural events organized in various ghettos could take on a larger meaning, as an affirmation of the dignity of daily life and hope for the future. Yitskhok Rudahshevski, a 15-year-old resident of the Kovno ghetto, commented on a party celebrating the circulation of the one hundred thousandth book in the ghetto library by observing, "The reading of books in the ghetto is the greatest pleasure for me. The book unites us with the future, the book unites us with the world."[4]

The Jewish struggle for survival in the ghettos was unique, but throughout Eastern Europe people had to decide how to respond to the challenges of occupation. Among them were those who, often motivated by a combination of anti-Semitism and material greed, turned on their Jewish neighbours. In Poland those who blackmailed and denounced Jews were very dangerous; in Warsaw some notorious youths were a constant danger to those still outside the ghettos. When the Germans invaded the Soviet Union in 1941 a number of Baltic peoples, Ukrainians, Belarusians, and Poles supported Nazi efforts to kill Jews.

There were other motives for collaborating with the Third Reich. Intense hatred of the Soviet system could nurture pro-Nazi sentiment. Some Baltic, Belarusian, Ukrainian, and Cossack activists, among them individuals who had previously lived for years in exile and had cultivated relations with Hitler's regime, hoped the overthrow of the Soviet system would pave the way for national freedom, though the Reich soon disappointed them on that score. For others cooperation was regarded as practical; in the Kalmyk region of the Soviet Union the population provided 3,000 cavalrymen and cattle for the German army in exchange for the re-opening of Buddhist temples and the reversion of some farmland to private use. Many civilians throughout Eastern Europe took jobs with the German military or civil administrations. Though doing so facilitated Nazi rule, these people saw their posts as ensuring survival for them and their families. Outside the workplace, relationships developed between German troops and local women, often in violation of racist regulations. In Ukrainian territory, for example, such liaisons were officially banned but often flouted; local women were drawn to occupying troops out of curiosity and for access to resources. Brothels reserved for the German troops were staffed by some prostitutes who worked voluntarily but also by women and girls forced to do so.

It did not take long for a growing number of East Europeans to become disaffected. By the fall of 1942 a German informer in Kiev reported that, whatever the terrors of Stalinist rule, people felt it was to be preferred to what the city was now experiencing: "Let the Bolsheviks return. They will shoot half of us, but the others at least will live and the misery will be over."[5]

To what extent people expressed their disaffection was another matter, for opposition was met with severe retribution. The assassination of Reinhard Heydrich, Heinrich Himmler's deputy and a key figure in implementing the Holocaust, illustrates this clearly. On 27 May 1942 Heydrich, who had recently taken over as the Protector of Bohemia and Moravia, was fatally wounded by British-trained Czech agents; he died a week later. The assassins were soon hunted down, and the Nazis wrought vengeance upon the general population. The villages of Lidiče and Ležáky were decimated for supposedly sheltering the agents. The men were shot, the women were deported to a concentration camp, and the children were taken for racial "screening," though most of them were later killed as well. Other Czechs accused of supporting resistance activities were executed. The total number of deaths in retribution for Heydrich's assassination reached 5,000. Later in the war the Czech government-in-exile in London grew concerned about the relative quiescence of the population, but in Bohemia and Moravia many people felt that further efforts to hinder the German war effort would only result in the deaths of innocents.

Despite the terrifying risks, people throughout occupied Eastern Europe and the Balkans still engaged in various forms of resistance. In Poland a large and sophisticated underground ensured the survival of national consciousness through encouraging a clandestine education system and set down a code of conduct for dealing with the Germans. It also supported Zegota, an organization established in 1942 that provided assistance to Jews by arranging for forged documents, hiding places, and food and medical care. Activities of this sort were not always so coordinated, but they were nevertheless significant. Yad Vashem, Israel's official Holocaust Remembrance authority, has identified over 22,000 individuals as "Righteous among the Nations," in recognition of their efforts to save Jews. Though the list is not exhaustive, it is worth noting that thousands of Poles, Ukrainians, and other East Europeans have been recognized.

The leading resistance organizations had political and military objectives. The Polish underground worked with the London-based government-in-exile, as well as the various nationalist militias that formed the Home Army (AK), which engaged in intelligence gathering, sabotage, and the punishment of collaborators. In Greece resistance also took on a mass character, but expressed a more radical political outlook, as the famine of 1941–42 served to discredit the country's political class. The Communist-led National Liberation Front (EAM) and its military wing, the People's Liberation Army (ELAS), combined patriotism with calls for a more egalitarian society and mobilized workers, women, and youth. Boldly protesting measures that affected ordinary peoples' lives, such as the conscription of workers for Germany, EAM/ELAS became a mass movement that dominated parts of the country.

Resistance movements were ideologically diverse, however, and sometimes rivalries between them were deadly. In Poland the Communist-led People's Army (AL) was relatively small, partly the result of its links to the widely hated Soviet Union; in contrast to the AK it was also more willing to engage German forces constantly and provoke reprisals, a feature of most Communist resistance organizations. In Greece the situation was reversed. There the Communist-inspired EAM/ELAS was in the ascendant, arousing opposition not only from the Germans and their Greek collaborators but also from a rival group, the strongly anti-Communist National Republican Greek League (EDES); the two movements actually came to blows in 1943–44. In Yugoslavia the Serb-dominated Chetniks were initially prominent foes of the Axis but became increasingly preoccupied with the growing influence of the Communist leader Tito (Josip Broz) and his Partisan movement. The two had very different political agendas—the Chetniks hoped to restore a Yugoslav monarchy in which Serbs played the leading role, while the Partisans sought to create a socialist and multinational state. Tito was also more willing to attack and risk retaliation from Axis forces than his Chetnik counterpart, Colonel Draža Mihailović. Early attempts at cooperation between the two soon broke down, and the Chetniks began cooperating with Axis forces, though Tito also entered into temporary negotiations with the Germans so that he could concentrate on fighting his domestic enemies.

Resistance in the occupied Soviet Union was powerfully conditioned by the fact that Stalin's regime remained intact. Partisan activity behind the German lines, involving stranded soldiers but also fleeing civilians, was increasingly directed by the government. One of the most spectacular actions by Soviet resisters was the assassination of Wilhelm Kube, the ranking Nazi official in occupied Belarus; in September 1943 he was blown up by a mine placed in his bed by his Belarusian maid. However, not all resistance groups in Soviet territory were coordinated by Stalin's regime. In parts of Ukraine nationalist militias were formed to oppose both the Germans and the return of Soviet rule; in other cases former collaborators of the Nazis switched sides as they grew disillusioned or increasingly aware of the likely outcome of the war. As German forces were driven out of the western borderlands of the Soviet Union in 1943–44, collaborators were frequently punished, but some nationalists in the Baltic States and Ukraine also resisted the return of the Red Army with guerrilla warfare.

Jewish resistance in Eastern Europe was necessarily of a distinctive character. Thousands of Jews evaded or escaped Nazi control, and while many fought as members of national partisan forces, some also formed their own separate groups. These included the Jewish Brigade led by Abba Kovner, which operated in the forests near Vilnius (Lithuania), and the group established by the Bielski brothers in occupied Belarus, which focused on survival and coexisted uneasily with other resistance formations, some of whose members harboured anti-Semitic views. In the ghettos, devastated by repeated deportations and widespread reports of death camps, elements of the community—often younger generations—made the case for armed resistance. There were revolts in some 20 ghettos, the most famous of which took place in Warsaw. Here the Jewish Fighting Organization led fierce resistance against German deportation operations for months, culminating in a fierce battle against 3,000 SS troops during April–May 1943. They were ultimately defeated—60,000 people in total died—but the insurgents realized from the start that victory was unlikely. Convinced that trying to hold on was futile, they decided to strike a blow against their tormenters and die with dignity.

Nazi Rule in Northern and Western Europe

German control in Northern and Western Europe was established very quickly, with the conquest of Denmark, Norway, Belgium, the Netherlands, Luxembourg, and France in the spring of 1940; the Nazis also occupied Britain's Channel Islands. As with Eastern Europe, a variety of occupation administrations existed. Denmark, a country whose population was of "Aryan stock" and had not offered significant resistance to invasion, was largely self-governing until 1943. In Norway, whose population was racially favoured, but which was strategically more vulnerable and had resisted the Germans strenuously, the Reich left a substantial occupation force. Belgium lost a small amount of territory to Germany, with the remainder being placed under military administration; the Netherlands, by contrast, was governed by a Nazi Party official. The case of France, a great power with the world's second-largest colonial empire, was particularly complex. The Germans annexed the region of Alsace and the department of the Moselle, and placed two northern departments under the control of their military officials in Belgium. German troops also occupied northern France and the country's Atlantic coastline, while Fascist Italy was allotted some territory in the southeast. The remainder of France, and its colonial empire, was to be governed by the newly installed government of Marshal Philippe Pétain, based in the spa town of Vichy. In foreign affairs, the Vichy regime sought favoured status in Hitler's New Europe through collaboration with Germany. Domestically, Pétain's government launched a "National Revolution," aimed at purging France of supposedly decadent elements— Marxists, Jews, and Freemasons—and promoting nationalist authoritarian values.

In the early stages of the occupation German troops in the north and west behaved with relative though not universal restraint, and Nazi officials did not have the same racist contempt for the locals; indeed, some were regarded as potentially valuable. But it would be wrong to downplay the difficulties the occupation caused. The Germans exploited local economies intensively. By 1943, for example, 40 per cent of France's output was being directed to the Reich, including 80 per cent of its vehicle production. Western Europe also supplied agricultural goods and workers. At first the latter were recruited voluntarily, but beginning in 1942 the Germans conscripted them in increasingly large numbers. Requisitions and frequently inadequate rationing meant that hunger and malnutrition were widespread, though massive famines like those that took place in the East were generally avoided. In terms of "racial policy," the Third Reich did not launch vast colonization schemes, but it did enforce Germanization in the territories seized from Belgium and France. Luxembourgers were also declared German citizens in 1942, with their younger men then being subject to conscription.

From the perspective of Northern and Western European civilians, the Nazi invasion caused considerable disruption, and the restrictions of the occupation unsettled social structures. Food and fuel shortages restricted people's consumption and travel, often leading to a narrowing of their social circles. Though the cinema also remained popular, in countries like Holland reading books and playing cards and board games within the family became more prevalent. The black market was a necessity to the point that it was often tolerated by local administrators and the Germans themselves, who sometimes resorted to buying outside legal channels to serve their own purposes. With large numbers of men absent—some 2 million Frenchmen alone were taken as POWs in 1940—women often found themselves thrust into new roles as decision-makers. Anne Somerhausen, the wife of a Belgian parliamentarian who had been captured, found herself left with her three sons. She was lucky enough to have office work and also rented out rooms, but by the summer of 1942 she was finding it impossible to make ends meet. She sold her appliances to raise cash; one profitable item was a Corona typewriter, which she sold to the German occupation authorities through a young intermediary, who made a tidy commission in the process.[6] Her experience shows the pressures that even relatively well-off people endured. The tragic case of a French mother of two, who hanged herself that same year and left a one-line note—"I am tired of standing in a line outside the market"—highlights the psychological implications of the constant struggle to obtain food.[7]

The Jews of Western Europe were singled out. Compared to Eastern Europe their communities were smaller and more integrated into the national culture, though there were important distinctions between individuals who had long been citizens of the country in which they lived and more recent immigrants, many of them refugees from Nazi persecution who now tragically found themselves within the Reich's grasp once again. German Jews, already in profound crisis before the war, suffered new restrictions from 1939 onwards; during the winter of 1941–42 they were even forced to surrender their winter clothes, supposedly for the sake of troops at the front. Though most Western European Jews were not subjected to ghettoization, discriminatory regulations—including removal from the professions, confiscation of their property, bans from restaurants and theatres, and most infamously the wearing of a yellow Star of David—were visited upon them. Vichy France did not impose the wearing of the star, but it had its own, home-grown anti-Semitic agenda, which mirrored that of the Nazis, stripping Jews of their civic equality and many recent migrants of their nationality. Raymond Raoul-Lambert, a French Jew who had been decorated for his service in the First World War, encapsulated the shock of persecution: "Thus can it be that in a few days I shall be a second-class citizen, that my sons, French by birth, culture, and faith will be brutally rejected from the French community.... Is it possible? I can't believe it. France is not France anymore."[8]

How did non-Jews respond to this persecution? A general strike was called in Amsterdam in February 1941 to protest the arrest of hundreds of Jewish men by the Germans, which spread to other cities before it was ruthlessly suppressed. But this incident was not typical. Although there was some sympathy for persecuted Jews, a fear of German repression, a fixation upon one's own needs, and the persistence of anti-Semitism meant that public reactions were generally muted. There was some commotion in France and elsewhere when the Germans began deporting Jews in the spring of 1942: even some who harboured prejudices regarded such measures as going too far. But scholars generally agree that active opposition was limited at this time.

When the time came to deport Jews, the Nazis secured the help of local bureaucracies and policemen, a fact that raises questions about the nature of collaboration. The most infamous collaborators—some historians use the term *collaborationist* to denote the political convictions they shared with the Nazis—were the local fascists. In Holland, Norway, and elsewhere such individuals served as administrators; in France they helped to hunt down resisters and Jews. But the Germans could not rely on them alone, as they had limited support in their own countries, and the Nazis regarded them as too nationalistic to be completely reliable. Even the Norwegian Fascist leader, Vikdun Quisling, who was installed as the head of a puppet administration, was regarded with some suspicion on these grounds. Other leaders of a less radical disposition, such as Marshal Pétain in France and Prime Minister Erik Scavenius in Denmark, the former a conservative nationalist with his own ideological agenda, the latter a veteran minister who saw himself as engaged in a balancing act between German demands and Danish sovereignty, were of great significance to the Nazis as partners. The civil servants, bureaucracies, and security forces who served them did so for diverse motives, but many of them believed they had to provide order, and more than a few, especially early in the war, were convinced that Hitler's European New Order would prove to be lasting.

Various elements of society also cooperated with the Germans. Businesses sought contracts from them to survive, though some firms were more enthusiastic than others. The French auto manufacturer Louis Renault adapted to producing for the German armed forces, while his counterpart Jean-Pierre Peugeot struck a deal with British intelligence whereby his firm would tolerate a degree of internal sabotage, an arrangement he made after the RAF bombed one of his factories. Tens of thousands of workers from various countries volunteered to go work in Germany, though they were often driven by economic need and the belief that opportunities awaited them, rather than strong political convictions.

The experience of women who engaged in sexual relations with occupation forces varied, though there were always perils involved. Even contact with German troops could be dangerous, as the fate of Rosina Povese demonstrates. Twenty years of age, she went to work for the Germans in France and in February 1944 found herself in a railway carriage with seven occupying troops; when she refused the advances of one of them, he killed her with a blow from his rifle butt.[9] The women who did develop liaisons with Germans were of various ages and backgrounds, but they tended to be young and had jobs, such as waitressing or assisting in a shop, that exposed them to the occupation forces. The motivations for the relationships that could ensue were often practical—connections with German troops might lead to a job or better access to provisions. But there could also be short-term romance and even lasting attachments. Significant numbers of children resulted from these unions: 12,000 to 16,000 in Holland and as many as 200,000 in France, according to one estimate. However, the consequences for women involved in or even accused of such relations were often dire, especially as the war came to a close. As we shall see, tens of thousands were harshly punished for their "sexual collaboration" during and after the period of liberation, and in some cases their children were ostracized.

While the majority of the occupied populations accommodated themselves to the Germans, and some went further than that, disaffection was also apparent. One early gesture of defiance came on 29 June 1940, when much of the Dutch population wore orange carnations in celebration of Prince Bernard's birthday, showing their patriotism. In France the 84-year-old Marshal Pétain initially enjoyed public respect, but as disillusionment with his regime set in jokes began to circulate: "Did you know the Marshal was dead? No. Since when? Three months ago, but his entourage have hidden it from him."[10] Strikes and demonstrations also took place. In the early stages of occupation they often had economic roots—miners in northern France and Belgium protested against deteriorating living standards in 1940–41, for instance. Yet while it may not have had an explicitly political focus, such discontent could lead the occupiers to make concessions. When the Germans tried to confiscate bicycles throughout Holland for their own use in 1942, the ensuing unrest—accompanied by other activities, such as listening to BBC broadcasts—led them to relent. They still officially restricted bicycle use to those who needed them for work, but they did little to enforce this rule.

The German policy of conscripting labour for the Reich, which came into force in 1942, did more than anything else to alienate civilians. The fact that it began at a point in the war when a Nazi victory seemed less likely, and when Allied bombing was starting to make Germany a very dangerous place to be, further intensified people's desire not to leave their own country. Hundreds of thousands did comply, unable to evade and sometimes feeling that they had no choice. In France, for example, labour conscription replaced obligatory military service and many young men, with fathers who had served in 1914–18 and/or were POWs in Germany felt it was their duty to go. Nevertheless, the policy evoked increasingly public opposition. In Belgium, where memories of a harsh German occupation during the First World War lingered, the Catholic Church spoke out; in Holland strikes broke out in the spring of 1943 when the population learned that the Germans intended to draft formerly interned Dutch soldiers. A minority of individuals avoided labour conscription by joining collaborationist groups, but more survived by assuming false identities and moving from job to job. In some rural areas evaders formed bands, the most famous of which were the French *maquis*.

There was thus a variety of negative responses to German rule, ranging from symbolic gestures, to protests aimed at specific measures, to organized resistance groups. Beyond expelling the Germans, the latter movements could have very different priorities. Some were politically quite conservative; at the opposite end of the spectrum, on the far left, there were the Communists, who were marginal in some countries but significant in Belgium and especially France. During the early years of the war the Nazi-Soviet Pact caused much confusion for Communists, as they were directed to criticize the British and French rather than the Germans. Following the invasion of the Soviet Union in 1941, however, Communist parties shifted to militant resistance against the Nazis. As in the East, their greater willingness to engage in attacks on German personnel and risk reprisals was controversial. Between these poles of conservatives and Communists were resisters who came from socialist or liberal backgrounds, or who had a religious orientation. There were also groups, like Norway's MILORG, that claimed to eschew politics and focused upon intelligence gathering and sabotage.

Though friction between different groups could be significant, full-scale clashes between resistance groups, akin to what occurred in the East, were less common in Western Europe. There tended to be a greater degree of cooperation, even if mutual suspicions never entirely disappeared. One example of growing integration was the creation of the Conseil National de la Résistance in France during the spring of 1943, whereby eight different movements accepted the leadership of General Charles de Gaulle, leader of the Free French movement based in London. In Denmark resisters of various stripes were represented on the Freedom Council. In Belgium, by contrast, the military-inspired Armée Secrète and the Communist-led Front de l'Indépendance never coordinated to such a degree.

The significance of resistance organizations grew as the war went on. They were behind many of the roughly 3,500 illegal newspapers started up in France, Belgium, Holland, Norway, and Denmark during the occupation. While some of these publications were very short-lived others achieved huge circulations, such as *Défense de la France*, which was printing over 400,000 copies by the winter of 1944. Resisters also engaged in sabotage, though such activities could lead to reprisals and a loss of public support; for instance, in 1943 thousands of Norwegians demonstrated *against* saboteurs who had wrecked a German troop train, because the occupying forces had responded by shooting five hostages.

Opposition groups ran rescue networks for Allied personnel, fugitives, and Jews, though there were also those who smuggled or hid people for profit. Perhaps 20,000 Jews reached neutral Switzerland or Spain via France in this way; a comparable number were sheltered in small, densely populated Holland. In an extraordinary feat involving resistance coordination but also the efforts of hundreds of ordinary people, the majority of the Danish Jewish community—over 7,000 people—was smuggled into Sweden on private boats in 1943.

For the civilians who engaged in them, resistance activities could have profound social and personal consequences. Members of the French *maquis* sometimes developed what British historian Rod Kedward has called an "outlaw culture."[11] They punished or killed collaborators and enforced ration quotas, but they sometimes also took from locals to meet their own needs, causing friction. Women played key roles in many groups, sometimes challenging traditional gender roles in the process. Though many female resisters engaged in the kinds of work one might expect at the time—securing food, providing medical care—the fact that they tended to arouse less suspicion than men, or could be regarded as attractive by a sentry, made them invaluable as couriers and liaisons. Some held leadership positions and even engaged in assassinations or combat operations. More than a few male resisters struggled with these changes, hesitating to acknowledge that their colleagues were truly "women." Juliette Dubois Plissonnier, a regional political organizer for the French Communist underground, recalled one occasion when, having arrived to chair a meeting, she was greeted by a male activist with the words, "What?! A woman here?" Another group member shot back, "She's not a woman, she's the boss."[12] However, as resistance groups become more highly structured in the later stages of the war, the exceptional women who did engage in combat operations were often reassigned to other duties as the desire to restore traditional gender roles intensified.

Resisters grew bolder as the war turned against the Germans. Though many movements avoided full-scale assaults, their attacks became more frequent. In France during the first nine months of 1943 there were assassination attempts against 281 Germans, 147 collaborators, and 97 police. In Holland over 40 local fascists, as well as other Dutch collaborators and Germans, were killed during a seven-month period that year. In Denmark, civilian government had remained in place until August 1943, but increasingly common strikes and sabotage led the Germans to declare martial law. A cycle of assassinations and reprisals followed, with German agents bombing a student hostel and the Royal Porcelain Factory in retaliation for a Danish raid on a *Wehrmacht* arms depot in Copenhagen; the Germans also carried out eight death sentences. As the aforementioned figures attest, by the final stages of the occupation, resistance to German rule also involved many clashes with collaborators, creating a civil-war atmosphere in some regions. In general, however, by the closing stages of the war ideological collaborators, always a minority, were increasingly isolated, while active resisters, though still only a small fraction of the population, enjoyed growing support.

Japan in East Asia

Though they already possessed colonies such as Taiwan and Korea, Japan's leaders denied that they were engaged in traditional empire-building. Instead, they asserted that as the most advanced of the Asian nations, Japan would provide leadership for what they called the "Greater East Asia Co-Prosperity Sphere." Their new satellite state of Manchukuo (the former Chinese province of Manchuria), formally established in 1932 with the former Chinese Emperor Pu Yi as its head of state, was held up as a model of how working with Japan would lead to prosperity, order, and harmony. A similar approach was pursued in the other Chinese territories that Japan conquered following the renewed assault begun in 1937 that resulted in the occupation of much of China's northern and coastal regions. Initially the Japanese experimented with different types of administrations but following the defection of Wang Jingwei, a rival of Jiang Jieshi within the GMD movement who became convinced that Japan would win, a new, puppet Chinese government was proclaimed under his leadership in 1940. This new "Reformed Government of the Republic of China" was supposed to work with Japan to combat the threat of Communism and to cast off Western influences. Wang died in 1944, but the regime and that of Manchukuo lasted until 1945, as did Japan's hold on Korea and Taiwan.

Rhetoric about fraternity notwithstanding, in reality Japanese control was always extensive, and so were Japanese demands for resources and labour. The whole system was also shaped by a widespread belief in the cultural, even racial superiority of Japanese to other Asians. In Taiwan and especially Korea, Japanese officials pushed rapid industrialization and promoted assimilation. These policies produced increasingly modern economies, but also communities that felt their identities to be under siege; eventually Taiwanese and Koreans were even compelled to adopt Japanese names. As for Manchukuo, it was to be a site for both industrialization and mass migration from Japan, to alleviate overcrowding and economic troubles. Japanese officials projected establishing 1 million households there within 20 years; the actual number of settlers by 1945 was around 300,000, but even with this lower figure vast numbers of local residents were displaced and had their land confiscated. In all cases, the local populations of occupied lands were drafted to provide labour for Japanese military and civilian projects and to provide industrial and agricultural goods as their imperial rulers saw fit.

Japanese rule certainly provided opportunities for some Asians, but it was ultimately based upon exploitation and force. Replicating policies on the home islands, from the late 1930s onwards colonial populations had to form patriotic associations in order to support the war effort of a regime that despoiled them economically and marginalized them culturally. Taiwan was more leniently administered than some possessions, but its population was profoundly affected by wartime mobilization. "In one week a farmer might be required to contribute a water buffalo to the Army, and in the next, representatives of the Navy might call on him to donate pigs, poultry, grain, or garden produce."[13] Young Taiwanese men were conscripted as labourers and came under increasing pressure to "volunteer" for the military as well; some 200,000 eventually served Japan in one capacity or another. Korea experienced even greater repression. Though Japanese-led industrialization provided opportunities for indigenous capitalists, created an urban workforce, and bequeathed the country with modern infrastructure, the demands made upon Koreans for goods and labour were cripplingly high. By 1941 there were some 1.4 million Koreans in Japan itself, many of whom laboured as construction workers or in manufacturing and mining. Another 4 million were mobilized for projects in Korea itself, and over 400,000 were drafted to serve elsewhere in the empire. A horrifying example of what could happen was the fate of some 7,000 Koreans drafted in 1944 to build an underground bunker near Mount Fuji for the Japanese imperial household. At least 1,000 died as they worked, many killed by reckless blasting aimed at clearing space for quarters and tunnels.

Life in the puppet state of Manchukuo also proved grim for most of the population. Propaganda themes that emphasized harmony among its different ethnic communities—Chinese, Mongol, Korean, Russian, and Japanese—obscured the realities of a racist and hierarchical system that favoured the latter. The presence of the Kwantung Army and the migration of Japanese settlers resulted in the resettlement of as many as 5.5 million local inhabitants to "collective hamlets," where overcrowding and disease were ever-present. Demographic restructuring on such a scale did not occur in the rest of Japanese-occupied China, but there too communities faced various requisitions and restrictions. Despite Japanese promises to be a force for order, crime remained a serious problem, as did opium addiction.

One of the most infamous features of Japanese rule involved the establishment of "comfort stations," through which tens of thousands of women became sex slaves. The stations were first established as official policy following the invasion of China in 1937; between 100,000 and 200,000 women were brought to them throughout the Japanese empire over the course of the war. The majority of the women came from Korea, but there were also Taiwanese and Chinese. Some were lured with misleading promises: others were simply abducted. Many comfort stations were located in battle zones, but even if they were not, all were inherently dangerous, as the testimony of one Korean former "comfort woman" makes clear:

> I was nearly killed several times during my time as a "comfort woman." There were some military men who were drunk and were brandishing swords at me while making demands for perverted sex.... The threat they were making was obvious—if I didn't cooperate they would stab me.[14]

The horrors of the system would be visited upon women in Southeast Asia when the Japanese invaded the region in 1941–42.

The Japanese needed a good deal of cooperation from the local population to make their empire run smoothly. Though the heads of puppet states such as Pu Yi and Wang Jingwei have naturally received much attention, Japanese officials also relied heavily upon local elites. They created "public order" committees, composed of influential members of the local community, to promote stability—under their close surveillance. The motivations of those who cooperated were sometimes complex. In the Chinese coastal city of Shaoxing, home to over a million people, the Japanese appointed Feng Xuzhou, a wealthy banker and head of the local chamber of commerce, as chief magistrate. Feng was put under considerable pressure by the Japanese secret service, who pointed to growing crime and disorder in the city. He eventually agreed to serve: it appears that he did so partly under duress, partly out of a sense of duty, but also possibly out of self-interest. As a banker his relations with the previous GMD regime had not been good, whereas for a time the banking sector in Japan-controlled Shaoxing prospered. Another important motivation for individuals like Feng was the perception that Japanese rule was likely to endure and would at least provide order in an era of upheaval.[15]

Those who opted to resist took fearsome risks. Japanese control in Taiwan and Korea was deeply rooted, buttressed by a mixture of political co-optation and ruthless repression, notably by the widely feared *Kempeitai*, Japan's military police. In Manchukuo there was at first substantial resistance to Japanese control. The number of guerrillas operating after the 1931 conquest might have been as high as 300,000, and they enjoyed moral and financial support from nationalist associations operating in northeast China. But in 1933 Jiang Jieshi signed a truce with Japan that renounced his government's claims to Manchuria and then banned anti-Japanese demonstrations relating to the region. This dampened support for the guerrillas, as did counterinsurgency efforts on the part of the Kwantung Army and Manchukuo collaborators. These sometimes involved brutal reprisals, such as the killing of nearly 3,000 men, women, and children near the city of Fushun in 1932 after a rebel attack killed several Japanese. Resistance in Manchuria, particularly on the part of Communists, was never extinguished, but it remained on the defensive. For example, the future Communist dictator of North Korea, Kim Il-Sung, led some partisan raids against the Japanese in both Manchuria and northern Korea between 1937 and 1940. The Japanese formed a special unit, made up mostly of former Korean insurgents, to track him down. Under severe pressure, Kim was eventually forced to retreat, taking refuge with his remaining followers in Soviet territory, though he continued to plan guerrilla operations and eventually returned to his liberated homeland in 1945.

At great cost, the Chinese Communist Party (CCP) slowly consolidated mass support among the peasantry of Japanese-occupied northern and central China. Such an achievement would have been scarcely predictable a decade earlier. In the 1920s the CCP had cooperated uneasily with the GMD, but after Jiang Jieshi assumed leadership of the Nationalists he turned on the Communists, decimating them. The CCP lost thousands more during its "Long March" to a stronghold in Shanxi province. However, the growing Japanese threat to China presented the Communists with opportunities. Increasingly dominated by Mao Zedong, the CCP called upon Jiang to form a "united front" against Japan. Initially the GMD leader refused, still regarding the Communists as his leading enemy, but in 1936 Jiang was kidnapped by a regional warlord and pressed to shift his policy. In 1937 he concluded an alliance with the CCP.

The alliance was unable to prevent Japan from seizing substantial amounts of territory in eastern China in 1937–38. However, the Japanese presence was uneven; it tended to be strongest in towns and cities and weakest in remote and mountainous districts. Especially after the fall of Wuhan in 1938, Communist activists, seeking to encourage guerrilla warfare and expand their movement, began to establish resistance "bases," primarily in rural areas behind the Japanese lines. They sought support from local populations through both social reform and political mobilization. In terms of social reform, CCP activists targeted exploitative landlords; often they would enforce a reduction in rents and/or interest payments. Efforts were also made to introduce cooperatives in some districts. Politically, the Communists established local committees to ensure order and formed elected assemblies to encourage popular involvement, though they lacked decision-making power. Activists also encouraged populations to rethink their roles in society and in some cases to challenge local class hierarchies.

Though the cumulative impact of these measures could be dramatic, it is important not to overstate the social changes that took place in the regions where the Communists established a presence. CCP activists, many of them urban intellectuals, had many difficulties—linguistic and cultural—in establishing connections with peasants. In some districts attitudes were quite conservative; Communist activists thus had to trim their propaganda and activities or risk alienation. For example, while Communists encouraged women to become more involved in public life in many districts, elsewhere they decided that such a course of action would offend too many locals. It should also be borne in mind that, while generally better disciplined and behaved than occupation forces, let alone the bandits who were endemic in some areas, the Communists had weaknesses. Their demands upon local populations could be deeply resented. In the Shandong region, where CCP activists had to contend with a strong Japanese presence and rival guerrilla activity from Nationalist supporters, internal party documents warned local cadres against "corrupting" themselves by confiscating property for personal use. The CCP could also be harshly intolerant of dissent: beginning in 1942 Mao launched a "Rectification Campaign" aimed at quashing potentially factious behaviour. This involved purges that ranged from public and humiliating "self-criticism" to torture and executions.

The CCP had to withstand frequent military pressure from the Japanese. After the Communists launched a major offensive in the autumn and winter of 1940, the Japanese and their Chinese collaborators responded with a counter-offensive featuring the "three-all" policy—"loot all, burn all, kill all." Giving the CCP no quarter and ravaging communities suspected of supporting it, the Japanese reduced the area under Communist control considerably. The size of the Communist forces dropped from 500,000 to 300,000 in 1941–42. However, as the war turned against Japan, especially from 1943 onwards, the situation eased somewhat, giving Mao and his supporters the chance to rebuild. By the end of the war the CCP had 1.2 million members and an army of similar size; it claimed to control a population of near 100 million.

Though the latter figure was likely exaggerated, the Communists were clearly in a far stronger position in relation to the Nationalists than they had been a decade before. The United Front had broken down during the war as clashes between the two sides had taken place, the most infamous of which was a large-scale Nationalist assault on Communist forces in January 1941. Total civil war was avoided thereafter, but as a Japanese defeat seemed more likely both sides tried to position themselves to dominate China after their common enemy surrendered. On paper, the GMD was still far stronger than the CCP in 1945, claiming the bulk of Chinese territory with a population of 350 million and an army three times as large as its rival. However, the shortcomings of the Nationalist war effort had cost Jiang's regime in terms of popular support. It would take an all-out effort in a subsequent civil war for the Communists to defeat the Nationalists, but their wartime expansion, paralleled by a hollowing of Nationalist enthusiasm, made it possible for them to do so.

Japan in Southeast Asia

Japan's expansion into Southeast Asia was a dramatic blow against Western colonial power. In the wake of the attack on Pearl Harbor, Japanese forces struck at British territories in the region, rapidly taking Hong Kong and Malaya. The conquest of Singapore in February 1942 was a humiliating defeat for Britain. To the west, British forces were also driven out of Burma by May, retreating to India. By then the vast Netherlands East Indies had also fallen, with the key island of Java being taken in March. Japan also conquered the US-dominated Philippines, with the last Filipino and American troops surrendering in May 1942. Japanese troops had been stationed in French Indochina since 1940, but they allowed pro-Vichy French officials to rule until March 1945, when they suppressed the French and created a short-lived puppet regime.

The Japanese empire presented itself as liberating Asians from Western colonialism, indicating that the new territories would take their place in the Co-Prosperity Sphere. A Ministry of Greater East Asia was established in November 1942, and conferences were held in 1943 and again in 1945 to project the image of a partnership. In reality the Japanese always retained control, though in some cases they relied upon local nationalists as puppets, while in other instances they governed more directly. In Burma they installed U Ba Maw, a well-known nationalist who had previously served as prime minister in cooperation with the British. Local nationalists also assisted the Japanese in conquering Malaya, but the new rulers subsequently deemed the Young Malay Union to be too radical and banned it, establishing a military administration instead. In the Netherlands East Indies the Japanese relied upon Dutch-trained civil servants, though they also secured the cooperation of Achmed Sukarno, a nationalist organizer and veteran of Dutch colonial jails. The Philippines had been dominated by the United States since 1898 but was transitioning to independence before Japan's attack. In 1942 the pro-US president, Manuel Quezon, went into exile; the Japanese army ordered Filipino civilian officials to keep working and established a collaborating "executive commission," headed by former Acting Chief Justice José Laurel.

Having established local administrations Japanese officials sought to mobilize anti-colonial sentiment throughout their new empire. In Indonesia the use of Dutch was abolished, and by 1943 mass organizations and rallies afforded Sukarno and other nationalists the chance to promote their ideas, stressing defence of the homeland and the need to resist any reassertion of Western control. Auxiliary military formations, such as PETA (Defenders of the Fatherland), were established to help oppose a possible Allied invasion; though its 38,000 members were not equipped with firearms, they did receive physical training. The Japanese-established Burma Defence Army fulfilled a parallel role, while propaganda from Tokyo and Ba Maw's government urged Burmese to be united, healthy, and disciplined. In Malaya the Malay population, women and schoolgirls as well as men and boys, took part in mass drills, parades, and gymnastics. Some Malays, such as Ibrahim bin Cheek, felt after the war that the Japanese had encouraged a sense of pride: "The Japanese period taught us [the Malays] to become more diligent, bad people did not dare do bad things, the spirit of love of country began because the Japanese always made the Malays aware of their rights in their own place."[16] In the Philippines Benigno Ramos was permitted to organize an auxiliary militia known as the Makapili, though Ramos's radical pro-Japanese outlook was unusual in his homeland, and the militia was not a great success. Even in French Indochina colonial officials followed the trend, encouraging patriotic mobilization. Tens of thousands of youths joined athletic associations and participated in sporting events. The Vichy Governor, Admiral Decoux, improved pay for Vietnamese civil servants and encouraged loyalty to an "Indochinese nation."

Japanese efforts to promote the Co-Prosperity Sphere as an anti-colonial alliance even extended to the granting of "independence" to Burma and the Philippines in 1943. By 1945 plans were in the works to do so in Indonesia as well. These largely symbolic gestures to convince other Asians that Japan was leading them away from colonial rule, however, were undermined by the heavy demands of the occupier. As a condition of Burma's "independence," Ba Maw was required to declare war on Britain and the United States; in the Philippines Laurel would have preferred not to but eventually did the same in 1944, working on the assumption that a victorious United States would be more forgiving than a desperate and likely vengeful Japanese empire (his calculation proved to be correct).

The costs of Japanese occupation went beyond political obedience. We have already seen the extent to which conscripted labour from Taiwan, Korea, and elsewhere was used; with the expansion of the empire came a concomitant increase in demand. In Vietnam the Japanese worked through the French colonial system of conscripting labour. In the Philippines local attitudes were conditioned by the impact of American trade unionism, which made for a more assertive workforce. Substantial numbers of Filipinos were pressed to work in mines, factories, and defence projects, but Japanese officials complained about a lack of cooperation. Indonesia, where the Dutch had long conscripted labour, now became a key source of workers for the Japanese, with as many as 4.1 million individuals drafted to work on various projects over the course of the occupation. Haji Mohammed Mukhandar, who provided Islamic funerals for workers who died working for the Japanese during the construction of a railway on the island of Java, recalled the situation during a 1979 interview:

Without human feeling the supervisors beat the workers when they saw them slack off in their work, or when they couldn't proceed because of exhaustion. The workers ate the remains of food, for which they fought, while the Japanese entertained themselves by throwing sand or water at them, laughing their heads off as if at a funny play.... Some workers were shot because they tried to run away, but far more died because of cruel tortures and unbearable suffering.[17]

Over 50,000 workers were transported to sites outside of Indonesia altogether, and some estimates suggest that over half of this group died, victims of harsh conditions, punitive treatment, and the perils of working in a war zone. Tens of thousands of conscripted workers from Burma and Malaya, along with thousands of Allied POWs, also met a grim end working on Japanese-initiated projects such as the Burma-Thailand railroad, where the mortality rate for labourers may have been as high as 39 per cent.

Though the Japanese were not interested in promoting industrialization in their newer possessions as they were in East Asia, they desired the rich natural resources of the region, such as Vietnamese rubber and Indonesian oil. Their procurement of such goods, plus the supply needs of their troops, quickly disrupted established trade relationships and undermined local agriculture. Burma was an exporter of rice, but the occupiers directed a shift towards cotton production. This disruption, plus the diversion of Burmese labour to other projects, led to a dramatic decline in rice cultivation: by 1945, 2 million acres of paddy land had become jungle. In the Philippines and Vietnam, Japanese demands for a shift from rice to cotton production similarly resulted in people going hungry. In Malaya occupation forces had, by contrast, encouraged a shift from rubber to food production to meet their particular needs. But the low prices that they set, and local fears that the Japanese would simply confiscate what they needed, meant that production still fell.

As was all too often the case in occupied territories, rationing and shortages gave rise to black markets, smuggling, theft, and above all hunger. By late in the war the situation was critical, exacerbated by the destruction of Japanese merchant shipping and bad weather in 1944–45. Japanese determination to keep stocks for their troops only made things worse; in May 1944 the occupation authorities for Malaya and Indonesia decreed a policy of bare subsistence for the local population. Malaya and Burma managed to avoid mass starvation, but living standards fell and medical care was in increasingly short supply. In some districts in both Indonesia and the Philippines deaths due to hunger and malnutrition became increasingly prevalent. The situation was most desperate in Vietnam, especially in the north. Rice was in short supply, and the margin of survival for many families was exceedingly thin, yet Japanese requisitions and stockpiling, often supported by the French administrators, continued apace. At least 1 million people—the Vietnamese Communists claimed twice that many—starved to death in the winter of 1945. One eyewitness captured the tragedy in poetry:

> Along all highways famished bodies moaned,
> lying curled up in the sun, in dust and filth.
> Amidst those rags the hollow eyes alone
> still harboured sparks of soul soon to go out.[18]

The relentless erosion of a tolerable existence was exacerbated by Japanese policies and attitudes in a host of ways. Comfort stations were established throughout the region, with young women from various national and ethnic backgrounds being lured or abducted to work in them, ranging from teenage Filipinas and Indonesians to some captured Australian nurses. Particular ethnic groups were singled out for harsh treatment; the 250,000 Dutch residents of Java, for example, were placed in internment camps. After the conquest of Malaya in March 1942 Japanese forces killed thousands of people from its ethnic Chinese community, claiming that these people had supported anti-Japanese activities in China itself; some of those killed included political activists, but young children were also among the victims. The community was also forced to pay 50 million (Malayan) dollars in "atonement" for its previous hostility to Japan.

Even in less extreme cases, the pervasive assumption of Japanese cultural superiority had a grave effect on everyday relations. For example, although it might seem a trivial issue, the fact that Japanese troops and officials frequently face-slapped other Asians (it was also inflicted upon subordinates in the Japanese military) became a source of tension. One Filipino official, who worked for the Japanese and considered himself an admirer of their culture—before the war he had taught Japanese history—nevertheless wrote a long paper on how to improve relations in which he warned the occupiers, "For heaven's sake stop this slapping business, once [and] for all. You just cannot understand, cannot fathom the depth of the resentment it causes, the amount of pain it gives to the victim."[19]

However, the path from resentment to active resistance was one that only a minority of people travelled. The emergence of opposition in Southeast Asia was also shaped by the complex dynamics of imperialism and nationalism in the region. Nationalists might judge it prudent to work with the

Japanese if the alternative was a return to European rule, though the changing fortunes of war could also lead them to reconsider. Communist movements gained support partly through their demands for social reform, but some kind of patriotic appeal was also crucial. Ethnic groups who sensed they had little future under Japanese domination tended to be earlier, more enthusiastic resisters. Such was the case for the Karen, Kachin, and Chin "hill tribes" of Burma, who feared oppression at the hands of the Burmese majority and looked to the British for protection. The Malaysian Communist Party (MCP) already had a disproportionately large Chinese membership before the invasion. Under the occupation the Japanese inclination to favour Malays and repress the Chinese intensified this trend. As with Communist movements throughout Europe and Asia, in an effort to appeal to a range of social classes as well as patriotic sentiment the MCP established a united front organization, the Malayan People's Anti-Japanese Union, and its military wing, the Malayan People's Anti-Japanese Army, which became the leading resistance movement in the peninsula. Though open to all ethnicities, given the dynamics of the occupation these organizations remained predominantly Chinese.

Resistance also emerged early in the Philippines, becoming significant by 1943. US influence was a factor here, as some stranded US soldiers fought in guerrilla bands. General MacArthur developed links with some resisters, among them supporters of President Manuel Quezon, who led a government-in-exile in Washington until his death in 1944. Although the US presence was far from universally popular, elements of the Filipino population—notably among the elite—had established a durable relationship with that country. The fact that the Philippines had been promised independence before the invasion reduced anxieties about renewed colonial domination after Japan had been defeated. Not all Filipino resisters shared this outlook; the Communist party established the Hukbalahap (People's Anti-Japanese Army), known simply as the Huks, which appealed to peasants on the basis of land reform and vigorous anti-Japanese resistance. By 1944 they had as many as 500,000 members and 30,000 fighting troops. But the Huks also faced formidable obstacles. As in Eastern Europe and elsewhere in Asia, the gap between non-Communist and Communist resistance often could not be bridged, and they soon engaged in clashes with anti-Communist resistance groups. Moreover, the Huks were regarded with intense suspicion by US forces, who returned to the Philippines in 1944.

In Vietnam Communist-led resisters were in a much stronger position. After the Indochinese Communist Party (ICP) attempted an uprising in

1940, French colonial authorities cracked down, and its remnants fled to southern China. Here, under the leadership of the Communist leader Ho Chi Minh, the League for the Independence of Vietnam (Viet Minh) was launched in the spring of 1941, seeking to unite different social groups and political movements against Japanese occupation and French colonial rule. The Viet Minh established a presence, especially in the north of the country, and expanded its appeal as famine spread in 1944–45. Its militants urged citizens to storm government and landlord granaries and began organizing raids itself, thus boosting its popular support. After the Japanese seized direct control in March 1945 they urged Bao Dai, who had previously served the French as a puppet emperor, to proclaim Vietnamese independence—an anti-colonial gesture that paralleled earlier sham declarations of independence in Burma and the Philippines. The Viet Minh had other plans. When the Japanese surrendered in August 1945 a power vacuum appeared, and Ho and his supporters reached for power throughout the country, declaring the formation of the Democratic Republic of Vietnam on 2 September. This was not the end of the story, though, for the French were determined to restore their presence in Indochina, by force if necessary.

In Burma and Indonesia Communists played a less prominent role; instead, nationalists who had initially worked with the Japanese but then grew disillusioned were the key catalysts, though there were major differences between the cases. The Burmese Defence Army (BDA), headed by the nationalist Aung San, was formed to support Japanese objectives, but worsening conditions in Burma, the growing likelihood of an Allied victory, and the poor treatment of its members by their Japanese colleagues led their leader to reconsider his position. By 1944 Aung San had developed contacts with the British and established the clandestine Anti-Fascist People's Freedom League to oppose the Japanese. As British imperial forces advanced back into Burma, the BDA switched sides and fought with them against the Japanese in the closing months of the war. In Indonesia, too, many nationalists had grown to hate the Japanese, though they did not wish to see the return of colonial rule. In February 1945 members of the Japanese-sponsored PETA militia rebelled. Yet the Indonesian nationalist leader Sukarno hesitated to break with Japan, despite increasing pressure from his supporters to do so. At one point they even kidnapped him to convince him, but in the end Sukarno went along with a Japanese-sponsored declaration of independence, though this did not actually occur until 17 August 1945, two days after the Japanese surrender. Sukarno's strategy was thus radically different from that of Aung San and especially Ho Chi Minh, but as the war drew to a close he too had established a foothold for independence, though this would only be fully attained after further struggle.

Conclusion

The impact of German and Japanese occupation was dramatic for millions of people. Exploitative demands and repressive policies soon led to growing discontent, organized opposition, and intensifying violence. Occupation was, in many ways, a profoundly divisive experience. The line between those who chose to cooperate and those who chose to resist sharpened as the war went on, though resisters often had diverging aims, with some seeking social revolution as well as national liberation. In Western Europe, such differences of opinion were generally, if uneasily, put aside in the service of a common cause. But in Eastern Europe the divisions between non-Communist and Communist resisters were more profound. This was also the case in East Asia, especially in China, where wartime conditions and evolving strategies strengthened the CCP in relation to the GMD. Japanese expansion also facilitated the unleashing of nationalist passions throughout Southeast Asia, to the point where European imperial power was permanently undermined, even though this was not always accepted at the time.

Further Reading

On German occupation policies, see Mark Mazower's *Hitler's Empire: How the Nazis Ruled Europe* (New York: Penguin, 2008). Studies of life in occupied Europe include Werner Rings, *Life with the Enemy: Collaboration and Resistance in Hitler's Europe 1939–1945* (New York: Doubleday, 1982); Rab Bennett, *Under the Shadow of the Swastika: The Moral Dilemmas of Resistance and Collaboration in Hitler's Europe* (New York: New York University Press, 1999); and Robert Gildea, Olivier Wieviorka, and Anette Waring, eds., *Surviving Hitler and Mussolini: Daily Life in Occupied Europe* (Oxford: Berg, 2006).

Accounts of European countries include Chad Bryant, *Prague in Black: Nazi Rule and Czech Nationalism* (Cambridge, MA: Harvard University Press, 2007); Richard Lukas, *Forgotten Holocaust: The Poles under German Occupation 1939–1944*, 2nd ed. (New York: Hippocrene Books, 1997); Mark Mazower, *Inside Hitler's Greece: The Experience of Occupation, 1941–1944* (New Haven, CT: Yale University Press, 1993); and Stevan Pawlowitch, *Hitler's New Disorder: The Second World War in Yugoslavia* (New York: Columbia University Press, 2008). On the Soviet Union, see Alexander Dallin, *German Rule in Russia 1941–1945*, 2nd ed. (Boulder, CO: Westview Press, 1981); Timothy Patrick Mulligan, *The Politics of Illusion and Empire: German Occupation Policy in the Soviet Union, 1942–1943* (New York:

Praeger, 1988); and Karel Berkhoff, *Harvest of Despair: Life and Death in Ukraine under Nazi Rule* (Cambridge, MA: Harvard University Press, 2004).

For France, see Richard Vinen, *The Unfree French: Life under the Occupation* (London: Penguin, 2006); Robert Gildea, *Marianne in Chains: In Search of the German Occupation of France 1940–45* (London: Pan Macmillan, 2002); and Julian Jackson, *France: The Dark Years, 1940–1944* (Oxford: Oxford University Press, 2001). For Holland, see Werner Warmbrunn, *The Dutch under German Occupation 1940–1945* (Stanford, CA: Stanford University Press, 1963); for Belgium, the same author's *The German Occupation of Belgium 1940–1944* (New York: Peter Lang, 1993); and for Norway and Denmark, Richard Petrow, *The Bitter Years: The Invasion and Occupation of Denmark and Norway 1940–1945* (New York: William Morrow, 1974).

There is a vast literature on the Holocaust. Short accounts include Doris Bergen, *War and Genocide: A Concise History of the Holocaust*, 2nd ed. (Lanham, MD: Rowman and Littlefield, 2009); Debórah Dwork and Robert Jan van Pelt, *Holocaust: A History* (New York: W.W. Norton, 2002); and Robert Wistrich, *Hitler and the Holocaust* (New York: Modern Library, 2001). Raul Hilberg's three-volume *The Destruction of the European Jews*, 3rd ed. (New York: Holmes and Meier, 2003) is a classic. Saul Friedländer, *The Years of Extermination: Nazi Germany and the Jews, 1939–1945* (New York: Harper Collins, 2007) is excellent.

For Japanese policies, see Peter Duus, Ramon H. Myers, and Mark Peattie, eds., *The Japanese Wartime Empire, 1931–1945* (Princeton, NJ: Princeton University Press, 1996); Yuki Tanaka, *Hidden Horrors: Japanese War Crimes in World War II* (Boulder, CO: Westview Press, 1996); Paul Kratoska, ed., *Asian Labor in the Wartime Japanese Empire: Unknown Histories* (Armonk, NY: M.E. Sharpe, 2005); and Yoshimi Yoshiaki, *Comfort Women: Sexual Slavery in the Japanese Military during World War II* (New York: Columbia University Press, 2000). For East Asia, see George Kerr, *Formosa: Licensed Revolution and the Home Rule Movement, 1895–1945* (Honolulu: University of Hawai'i Press, 1974); Bruce Cumings, *The Origins of the Korean War: Liberation and the Emergence of Separate Regimes, 1945–1947* (Princeton, NJ: Princeton University Press, 1981); and Rana Mitter, *The Manchurian Myth: Nationalism, Resistance, and Collaboration during the Manchurian Crisis, 1931–1933* (Berkeley, CA: University of California Press, 2000). On China, see David Barrett and Larry Shyu, eds., *Chinese Collaboration with Japan, 1932–1945: The Limits of Accommodation* (Stanford, CA: Stanford University Press, 2001); and Timothy Brook, *Collaboration: Japanese Agents and Local Elites in Wartime China* (Cambridge, MA: Harvard University Press, 2005). On the rise of the Chinese Communist party, Lyman Van Slyke's "The Chinese Communist Movement during the Sino-Japanese War, 1937–1945," pp. 177–290 in Lloyd Eastman *et al.*, eds., *The Nationalist Era in China 1927–1949* (Cambridge: Cambridge University Press, 1991) is an excellent introduction. There are recent case studies in Feng Chongyi and David Goodman, eds., *North China at War: The Social Ecology of Revolution, 1937–1945* (Lanham, MD: Rowman and Littlefield, 2000).

For Southeast Asia, see Nicholas Tarling, *A Sudden Rampage: The Japanese Occupation of Southeast Asia, 1941–45* (Honolulu: University of Hawai'i Press, 2001); Alfred McCoy, ed., *Southeast Asia under Japanese Occupation* (New Haven,

CT: Yale University Southeast Asia Studies, 1980); and Christopher Bayly and Tim Harper, *Forgotten Armies: Britain's Asian Empire and the War with Japan* (London: Penguin, 2004). For Malaya, see Paul Kratoska, *The Japanese Occupation of Malaya: A Social and Economic History* (Honolulu: University of Hawai'i Press, 1997); and Cheah Boon Kheng, *Red Star over Malaya: Resistance and Social Conflict During and After the Japanese Occupation, 1941–1946*, 2nd ed. (Singapore: Singapore University Press, 1987). Theodore Friend, *The Blue-Eyed Enemy: Japan against the West in Java and Luzon, 1942–1945* (Princeton, NJ: Princeton University Press, 1988) is a comparative study. David Marr, *Vietnam 1945: The Quest for Power* (Berkeley, CA: University of California Press, 1995) is fascinating.

Notes

1   Quoted in Michael Burleigh, *The Third Reich: A New History* (New York: Hill and Wang, 2000), 442.

2   Quoted in Richard Evans, *The Third Reich at War* (New York: Penguin, 2008), 351.

3   See Debórah Dwork and Robert Jan van Pelt, *Holocaust: A History* (New York: W.W. Norton, 2002), 222–23.

4   Quoted in Alexandra Zapruder, ed., *Salvaged Pages: Young Writers' Diaries of the Holocaust* (New Haven, CT: Yale University Press, 2002), 217–18.

5   Quoted in Karel Berkhoff, *Harvest of Despair: Life and Death in Ukraine under Nazi Rule* (Cambridge, MA: Harvard University Press, 2004), 224.

6   As recounted in Aldrich, ed., *Witness to War*, 462–63.

7   Quoted in Richard Vinen, *The Unfree French: Life under the Occupation* (London: Penguin, 2006), 215.

8   Quoted in Saul Friedländer, *The Years of Extermination: Nazi Germany and the Jews, 1939–1945* (New York: Harper Collins, 2007), 120.

9   See Vinen, *The Unfree French*, 180.

10 Quoted in Julian Jackson, *France: The Dark Years, 1940–1944* (Oxford: Oxford University Press, 2001), 283.

11 See H.R. Kedward, *In Search of the Maquis: Rural Resistance in Southern France 1942–1944* (Oxford: Clarendon Press, 1993), esp. 56–57, 95–101.

12 Quoted in Paula Schwarz, "*Partisanes* and Gender Politics in Vichy France," in Gordon Martel, ed., *The World War Two Reader* (New York: Routledge, 2004), 302.

13 George Kerr, *Formosa: Licensed Revolution and the Home Rule Movement, 1895–1945* (Honolulu: University of Hawai'i Press, 1974), 194.

14 Yuki Tanaka, *Hidden Horrors: Japanese War Crimes in World War II* (Boulder, CO: Westview Press, 1996), 99.

15 See R. Keith Schoppa, "Patterns and Dynamics of Elite Collaboration in Occupied Shaoxing County," in David Barrett and Larry Shyu, eds., *Chinese Collaboration with Japan, 1932–1945: The Limits of Accommodation* (Stanford, CA: Stanford University Press, 2001), 167–68.

16 Quoted in Paul Kratoska, *The Japanese Occupation of Malaya: A Social and Economic History* (Honolulu: University of Hawai'i Press, 1997), 348.

17 Quoted in Harry Poeze, "The Road to Hell: The Construction of a Railway Line in West Java during the Japanese Occupation," in Paul Kratoska, ed., *Asian Labor in the Wartime Japanese Empire: Unknown Histories* (Armonk, NY: M.E. Sharpe, 2005), 164.

18 Quoted in David Marr, *Vietnam 1945: The Quest for Power* (Berkeley, CA: University of California Press, 1995), 105.

19 Quoted in Theodore Friend, *The Blue-Eyed Enemy: Japan against the West in Java and Luzon, 1942–1945* (Princeton, NJ: Princeton University Press, 1988), 144.

3 | The Impact of Violence

As many as 60 million people died as a result of the Second World War; over half of them were civilians. In some cases these deaths were the unintended, though not necessarily unanticipated, by-product of military operations, but non-combatants were often deliberate targets. Hoping to cause panic, invading armies attacked population centres and fleeing refugees. Rampaging troops frequently robbed, assaulted, and murdered non-combatants. One of the defining characteristics of the Second World War was the mass bombing of civilians, which was intended not only to disrupt the war effort but also the cohesion of enemy populations. These attacks killed hundreds of thousands and culminated in the use of atomic weapons. In many cases civilians were killed to promote military objectives, but in the case of the Nazi quest to annihilate Europe's Jews, the destruction of an entire people was the end in itself.

To the very final stages of the war, civilian populations were engulfed by violence—indeed, the destruction intensified over time. In some cases non-combatants had to fear not only the enemy but also their own governments, if the latter were bent upon terrorizing their own people in order to ensure continued resistance against invaders. The civil war between resisters and collaborators, which emerged in some occupied regions, frequently engulfed people who did not want to get involved. However, not all civilians were passive bystanders or victims; many engaged in violence against foreigners or fellow citizens.

No brief synopsis can hope to encapsulate the horrors and psychological damage wrought upon those caught in the maelstrom of the Second World War. What can be suggested, however, is that while the destruction of civilian morale and social cohesion was often a goal, such an objective was achieved only in certain cases. Attacks upon non-combatants often bred fear and trauma, sometimes leading to collapse. But cycles of violence could also evoke determination and hatred, fuelling defiance and resistance. Moreover, the social upheavals that accompanied mass violence against civilians, though often involving breakdown, could also promote desires with longer term implications not only for radical social and political change in some cases but also for peace, stability, and renewal. Both impulses would shape the aftermath of the war.

Invading Armies

Chinese citizens had very good reasons to fear the invading Japanese army, which was capable of major atrocities towards non-combatants. The most infamous slaughter took place following the Japanese capture of the GMD regime's capital of Nanjing in December 1937, an event often known as the "Rape of Nanking." Many Japanese soldiers, who operated under a regime of brutal discipline, already held the Chinese people in contempt. Chinese resistance in the early stages of the battle was unexpectedly fierce, provoking Japanese anger over their losses. The fact that the commander of Nanjing's defenders later fled, leaving his troops in disarray, added to the chaos. Japanese troops, having fought hard, and faced with having to forage for supplies amongst a population whom many of them despised, engaged in a wave of killings. Some of these were "justified" on the grounds that the invading troops faced potential resistance from Chinese soldiers now disguising themselves as civilians, but it appears that many of those men no longer had any taste for battle and simply wished to survive. In addition, thousands of POWs were executed, and troops engaged in plunder, rape, and murder of civilians on a scale that soon gave their commanders cause for concern.

The Nanjing Massacre remains a subject of great controversy. Contemporary Japanese nationalists downplay the figures, and some even deny that a massacre took place. Conversely, some Chinese accounts imply that the Imperial Army intended genocide. Estimating the number of victims depends on how scholars define the geographical and chronological limits of the massacre, as well as the issue of whether deserting soldiers out of uniform should be counted as victims alongside non-combatants. Some estimates are as high as over 300,000 people, though it has been argued that this figure more accurately reflects total Chinese military and civilian deaths from the time of the initial Japanese attack until the taking of the city. More conservative reckonings of Chinese deaths at Nanjing fall between 100,000 and 200,000, and some are even lower than that. What is beyond dispute is that tens of thousands of Chinese civilians lost their lives, and many experienced ridicule, torture, and repeated sexual assault before being killed.

The ordeal of the Chinese people hardly ended with Nanjing. To take one horrifying example, the capital of Hunan province, Changsha, was the target of four major Japanese offensives between 1939 and 1944, the last of which finally took the city; an estimated 150,000 Chinese died in the process. Some defensive measures by Jiang Jieshi's regime also proved deadly. Efforts to slow the Japanese advance by breaching the dykes of the Yellow River in 1938 led to as many as 400,000 Chinese, as well as an unknown number of Japanese, deaths. After that year the Japanese advance slowed somewhat, but the killing continued. Japan forces allegedly used chemical and biological weapons when they carried out attacks in Chekiang and Kiangsu provinces in retribution for the Doolittle Raid, a small-scale, though psychologically significant, US bombing attack on Tokyo carried out in April 1942. Chinese civilians and POWs, along with Koreans and possibly some Western prisoners, were used as live biological warfare test subjects by Japan's Unit 731, based in Harbin, Manchuria. Communities such as the hamlet of Chongsan were reportedly exposed to bubonic plague.

As we have seen, some regions of Japanese-occupied China were relatively calm, but elsewhere operations to stamp out ongoing Chinese resistance, whether Communist or Nationalist, led to civilian deaths on a massive scale. The destruction Japanese troops—sometimes supported by Chinese collaborators—wrought was immense. However, they found it very difficult to totally extinguish resistance operations, and in some cases they encouraged local opposition to their presence. A comment by the American journalist Theodore White captures both the devastation and consequences of Imperial Japanese policy: "From one end of northern China to another the black shells of villages gave testimony to the wrath of the enemy, while in a hundred thousand homes peasants nursed the bitterness of revenge for a wife raped, a husband tortured, a child slaughtered in cold blood."[1]

Beginning in 1941–42 the populations of Southeast Asia faced Japanese onslaughts. Though the loss of civilian life was not on the scale of China, as there were fewer battles in densely populated urban areas, there were various atrocities. In Singapore units of the Imperial Army executed between 5,000 and 10,000 ethnic Chinese; thousands more were killed in Malaya. The Japanese conquest of Hong Kong was followed by a chaotic rampage. Massacres also took place in the Philippines and Indonesia; in the latter case the Japanese punished Dutch inhabitants for destroying oil fields by carrying out executions and engaging in sexual assaults. As in occupied China, resistance in Southeast Asia was punished with harsh reprisals. The cycle of violence was particularly intense in the Philippines: the postwar Tokyo war crimes tribunal estimated that 91,184 Filipino citizens were murdered or starved to death during the occupation.

The propensity of the German armed forces to engage in atrocities against civilians quickly became apparent during the invasion of Poland in 1939. The campaign itself was relatively brief but characterized by intense fighting; the fact that local ethnic Germans were murdered by Polish troops and civilians—the exact number is uncertain—inflamed German anti-Polish hostility. So did the tenets of Nazi racism and the propaganda of Joseph Goebbels, which exaggerated the number of German victims. Between the start of the invasion on 1 September and the final subjugation of resistance on 5 October 1939, German forces executed some 16,000 civilians. As we have seen, among these victims were members of Poland's educated elite and its Jewish community. Instrumental to their murders were the *Einsatzgruppen* (task forces), mobile killing squads under SS command, tasked with eliminating political and racial enemies of the Reich. First deployed during the German takeover of Austria in 1938, the *Einsatzgruppen* were a key instrument of Nazi terror in Poland, and would be again in the Soviet Union.

But they did not operate alone. *Wehrmacht* (German armed forces) commanders also had the power to take hostages and carry out "preventative" executions to deter guerrilla resistance, and many did not hesitate to do so. The recollections of Wladyslawa Bera, an inhabitant of the village of Widzów in western Poland, give an indication of how these operations unfolded. As German forces moved through her village on 4 September 1939 they ordered the local men to assemble in the street, even though other witnesses testified that there had been no previous civilian opposition to the invaders. Bera's husband and stepson were among those who obeyed the summons. Subsequently,

The men were surrounded and ordered to raise their hands. They were driven to a site near the fire station and stood up against a fence. I ran to them to save my husband, threw my arms around him and begged for his life. I was eight months pregnant at the time, but a German kicked me. I fell and lost consciousness. When I awoke the execution was over. I saw the bodies of the thirteen dead men. The Germans were no longer there ... my stepson was only fifteen years old.[2]

Under such circumstances it does not seem surprising that resistance organizations quickly began to appear in Polish territory.

Many of these patterns were repeated on an even greater scale during the invasion of the Soviet Union in 1941. Widespread belief in the inferiority of Slavic peoples, heightened by fanatical Nazi anti-Communism, ensured that Soviet populations suffered immensely. From the start of Operation Barbarossa villages were bombed and burned, suspected insurgents shot out of hand, and murderous punishment meted out to communities suspected of harbouring guerrillas. However, some German officers soon discerned that these policies were failing to cow the majority of the civilian population or the Red Army. Writing to his wife on 22 July 1941, one month after the invasion began, General Gotthard Heinrici commented that, "One does not have the feeling that in general the Russian will to resist has been broken, or that the people want to drive out their Bolshevik leaders. For the moment one has the impression that the war will go on, even if Moscow is taken, somewhere in the depths of this endless land."[3]

The experiences of the citizens of Leningrad, who withstood a siege that lasted from October 1941 until January 1944, illustrate the catastrophes that Soviet civilians experienced but also their determination to resist the invader. During the first and most terrible winter of the siege, in 1941–42, the situation was dire; food shortages led to widespread malnutrition and mass starvation. The social fabric of the city reached its breaking point; some resorted to crime, even cannibalism, in order to survive. Considerable resentment sprang from well-founded accusations that Communist party officials and other elites had privileged access to food. Yet the city held on. The forces of social disintegration were outweighed partly by significant state repression—the NKVD carried out executions in order to quash petitions for the city's surrender—but also by patriotism, hatred of the Germans, and a simple determination to persevere. Consider the story of Yelizaveta Sharypina, a schoolteacher and Communist party worker, who lived through the siege. Her children had been evacuated from the city, but she and her husband Pavel remained. Food was very scare, to the point that Pavel, who had previously referred to Yelizaveta as "my better half," now called her "my little quarter" because she had grown so thin. The couple had to make the most of whatever luck came their way during that first winter of the siege:

> There was a surprise for New Year's: an hour or two of electric light. And another surprise: [Yelizaveta] had traded two dresses for a pound or two of sausage (better not to ask what kind) and a pound of horse meat. She and Pavel had saved their bread ration until evening, and she had put away five pieces of soya candy. They had a real New Year's feast.[4]

Leningrad held on, but the price its people paid was shocking. Out of a prewar population of nearly 3 million, only 639,000 were left in the city by March 1943, nearly a year before the siege finally ended. Some 850,000 people had been evacuated, and the Soviets officially listed 632,253 civilians as having been killed. That leaves a figure of approximately 1 million people, more than the combined military and civilian casualties of Britain and the United States, unaccounted for. Many of those people likely starved during the winter of 1941–42.

The dynamics of the Third Reich's invasion of Western Europe in the spring of 1940 were different. Hitler and his colleagues sought a quick victory and an orderly, profitable occupation, with fewer sweeping plans for racial "restructuring." Initial German attacks provoked a massive flight of refugees, first from Holland, then Belgium, and finally northern France in a cataclysm likened by one contemporary to the barbarian invasions of the fourth century. Millions streamed southwards; they were joined by military stragglers, mostly from a French army in the midst of disintegration. This flight attracted enemy attention, and German aircraft bombed and strafed columns of refugees as well as railway stations. The results of one such attack were captured in stark terms by the French academic André Morize:

> I saw and touched the lacerated cars. I saw blood on the cushions of the seats. I saw the car from the Ardennes and among the bundles and the cases, rolled up in blankets was the body of a little girl whose father was looking for a cemetery. I saw a 10-year-old boy whose shoulder was fractured by a bullet. I saw a woman who hardly knew how to drive at the wheel of an old Renault taking her three children away with her because her husband was killed on the road in the Pas-de-Calais.[5]

As many as 100,000 civilians died in the course of the exodus, victims of attacks as well as accidents. Though the individual experiences of refugees varied—those with means were often better able to cope, and not all columns were attacked—the refugee flight provoked a widespread sense of disorientation and fear of social breakdown. While some plans for evacuation existed, and many towns and cities in southern France did their utmost to welcome and comfort refugees, there were also instances where they were turned away or robbed. Many citizens felt that their leaders had let them down, even abandoned them.

As hostilities came to an end, both the German conquerors and the new Vichy regime capitalized upon this resentment and insecurity in a quest for public support. Marshal Pétain explicitly appealed to the millions of refugees, promising them safety and a return to their homes. His message resonated with a frightened populace. Simultaneously, the German military quickly shifted gears to portray itself as eager to help. Propaganda denigrated the failure of France's democratic leaders and encouraged the public to look to German soldiers for aid. Avoiding much of the blatant racism so previously on display in Poland, and later evident in the Soviet Union, German troops were directed to show restraint and encourage people to return home. Their goal was to discourage discontent and guerrilla activity; in this regard they proved to be quite successful in the opening months of the occupation.

Racial Atrocities and Genocide

Racist attitudes incited many wartime atrocities against civilians. Though most historians avoid using the term "genocide" in connection with Japanese goals during the fighting in China and the Pacific War, there can be no doubt that contempt for other Asians and a desire to humiliate Westerners were key motivations. Conversely, anti-Japanese racism led to the internment of tens of thousands of people in North America and encouraged a de-humanization of the enemy on the part of US and British Commonwealth forces. But it was in Europe that racism led to a systematic campaign to annihilate an entire people.

By the time of the German-led invasion of the Soviet Union in 1941, Jews throughout Nazi-occupied Europe had already been subject to violence, harsh restrictions, and humiliation. But it was with the attack on the Soviet Union, an operation that Hitler viewed in apocalyptic terms, that the decision to murder the Jews of Europe unfolded. The *Einsatzgruppen* were directed to eliminate various Communist officials and potential resisters. Since in the Nazi world view Jews were at the heart of the Bolshevik system, they were defined as deadly enemies, deserving of pitiless extermination. Many German generals relayed brutal instructions to their troops, urging them to be merciless. As the *Wehrmacht* steamrolled through the western Soviet Union in the summer and fall of 1941, *Einsatzgruppen*, other police formations, and army units, sometimes assisted by auxiliaries from the local population, engaged in mass killings. At first they targeted men of military age, but before long they included women and children, and then entire communities, in the slaughter. The following eyewitness account from the Jewish village of Cherikov, located in present-day Belarus, suggests how events unfolded:

> The Hitlerites arrived ... on July 16, 1941. After beginning with isolated shootings of unarmed civilians, the Germans then proceeded to mass killings and shootings. In October 1941, the Hitlerites announced the "resettlement of the entire Jewish population to another locality." Approximately five hundred Jews were herded into the [local town hall].... The soldiers opened fire with submachine guns on the defenceless crowd that was speechless with fear. The Germans did not leave until they had wiped out every last one of the five hundred Jews.[6]

Scenes such as this were repeated all over the occupied territory in the opening months of the invasion. Germany's allies, notably Romania, also participated in the genocide. Even before the invasion Romanian fascists had engaged in a brutal pogrom against Bucharest's Jewish community; during Operation Barbarossa the same country's soldiers were responsible for, among other murders, killing 30,000 Jews in the city of Odessa. Historians estimate that by the end of 1941, 1 million Jews in the occupied Soviet Union and Baltic States had been killed. By then German forces had also murdered thousands of Jewish men in Serbia.

Mass shootings by various German forces and foreign helpers claimed another 700,000 Jewish deaths the following year. By this time other methods of killing were also in use. The Nazis established their first death camp, Chelmno, in December 1941. Its victims were killed in specially modified vans, which redirected carbon monoxide fumes from the exhaust back into the cargo compartment, asphyxiating them. In the months that followed additional killing centres, equipped with gas chambers, were opened at Belzec, Sobibor, Treblinka, and Madjanek. Like all of these camps, the most infamous one, Auschwitz, was located in occupied Polish territory. It had initially been established as a forced labour camp, but it was also equipped with gassing facilities in 1942. By the summer of that year the camps were fully operational; by the end of December 1.5 million men, women, and children, most of them Jews from the General Government

(Nazi-controlled Polish territory), had perished in them. Indeed, the Nazi-orchestrated killing campaign in 1941 and 1942 was so intense that at the beginning of 1943 three-quarters of the approximately 6 million victims of the Holocaust were already dead.

Some of Germany's allies, such as Romania, became less willing to cooperate in the genocide as the fortunes of war shifted. Nevertheless, deportations continued, from as far away as France to the west and Greece and Italy to the south. In the spring and summer of 1944, as the German war effort entered its terminal crisis, the Nazis devoted considerable time and resources—with help from various Hungarian officials and anti-Semites—to rounding up over half (440,000 out of 725,000) of that country's Jewish population and sending them to Auschwitz. When Admiral Miklos Horthy, the regent of Hungary, ordered a halt to the deportations following intense international pressure, he was overthrown at German instigation and replaced by a fascist puppet regime, supporters of which soon engaged in mass shootings of Budapest's Jewish population.

Faced with a powerful, ruthless enemy, initially unsure of what was happening, and often isolated from other communities, many European Jews had little chance to respond, let alone determine their fate. Fleeing, joining partisan groups, or seeking shelter with non-Jews were sometimes options, but all entailed enormous risks and were only possible for a fraction. The Nazis and their allies also made constant use of deception. Jews were often told that they were going to be relocated and used for labour rather than killed. This tactic was employed not only in cases of mass shootings but in deportations to the camps as well. Even people who had heard rumours about death camps understandably resisted believing them. Etty Hillesum, who lived in Amsterdam, noted in July 1942 that, "The Jews here are telling each other lovely stories: They say that the Germans are burying us alive or exterminating us with gas. But what is the point of repeating such things, even if they should be true?"[7] She was deported to, and murdered in, Auschwitz the following year.

During the deportations people were stuffed into railway cars with little food, heat, or sanitation; some perished even before reaching the camps. When they arrived at their destination the camp authorities aimed to shock them into submission. As Primo Levi, whose haunting account of his time in Auschwitz is one of the most influential memoirs of the Holocaust, recounted, "The door opened with a crash, and the dark echoed with outlandish orders in that curt, barbaric barking of Germans in command which seems to give vent to millennial anger.... In less than ten minutes all the fit men had been collected together in a group. What happened to the others, to the women, to the children, to the old men, we could establish neither then nor later: The night swallowed them up, purely and simply."[8] Levi later discovered that over 500 of the roughly 625 people he had been deported with were immediately sent to the gas chambers. In order to facilitate the killing, victims were typically told that they simply had to take a shower in order to be disinfected.

Since the vast Auschwitz complex was a labour camp as well as a killing centre, some deportees were kept alive, at least for a time, to be exploited for their labour. They suffered food shortages, tattered clothing, disease, infestation, and all-encompassing arbitrary brutality; some inmates were also subjected to gruesome medical "experiments." The prisoners were segregated by gender, and Jews of different nationalities and languages were forced together, overseen sometimes by Jews but also other political and criminal prisoners. Under these conditions, suicides were common, especially among the recently deported. Nor is it surprising that focusing on one's own survival could lead to a lack of solidarity with other prisoners, while the exhausting challenges of everyday survival tragically engulfed some individuals, who grew resigned to their fate before they succumbed to malnutrition or were sent to the gas chambers.

Yet the Nazi quest to destroy the spirit as well as the bodies of the Jews was often contested to the bitter end. There were numerous escape attempts, both from the deportation trains and from the camps themselves. Prisoners chosen to labour, or to assist in the running of the camp, had the chance to forge bonds, and in some cases this led to rebellion. Underground groups staged uprisings in both Treblinka and Sobibor in 1943. In the latter case they succeeded in killing 11 guards, and some 300 people escaped, though one-third of them were quickly caught and shot, and most were eventually recaptured. In October 1944 members of the Jewish *Sonderkommando* (special commando) in Auschwitz, who were tasked with the removal of bodies after gassing, staged a revolt and succeeded in destroying one of the crematoria before attempting their escape; 250 prisoners were killed in the uprising, and another 200 were executed in reprisal. Defiance could even be expressed in death, as the case of Mala Zimetbaum illustrates. A Jewish girl of Polish origin who had been sent to Auschwitz from Belgium, she and a male prisoner managed to escape for two weeks before being recaptured: both were sentenced to hang. However, Mala cut her wrists just before the execution itself and slapped the face of her SS escort. By doing so she avoided the spectacle of a hanging and instead died in the gas chamber.[9]

Though the Nazis regarded the Jewish people as their primordial enemy, the camp system claimed vast numbers of other victims. These included hundreds of thousands of political opponents, as well as people guilty of "asocial" activities criminalized by the Reich. Many of them did not survive; some, such as homosexuals, were frequently ostracized by their fellow prisoners and suffered particularly high mortality rates. Nazi plans for the "purification" of Germany and the racial restructuring of Europe also led to the killing of the physically and mentally disabled, both in the Reich itself and in the occupied lands. A program to secretly eliminate disabled children had been put into motion in 1939, and Hitler soon approved one for adults. This killing operation, codenamed "T-4," involved selecting asylum patients who were then killed by a variety of means, including lethal injection and gassing. Some of these methods, and some of the personnel, would later be involved in killing Jews. Following the outbreak of war the murder of the disabled spread eastwards. During the fall of 1939, for instance, German forces killed inmates in Polish asylums. In the Reich itself, growing suspicions by some of the victims' families culminated in public criticism of the Nazi regime by the Catholic Bishop of Münster, Cardinal August Count von Galen, in August 1941. Hitler responded to the discontent by proclaiming a halt to the program, but in fact the killings continued in secret.

The Nazis also decimated the Roma, or "Gypsy," population of Europe. Long the targets of persecution in many countries, in Nazi Germany Roma were regarded as social undesirables who were also racially problematic. SS leader Heinrich Himmler eventually decided that a proportion of "racially pure" individuals should be preserved as subjects of further study, because he believed they were linked to the original Aryans. But most Roma, and those of mixed descent as well as itinerants who shared their lifestyle, were labelled troublesome degenerates, and from 1938 onwards those living in the Reich faced increasingly severe penalties. During the war German security forces executed thousands in Poland, the Soviet Union, and Serbia, and thousands more perished in various camps, notably Auschwitz, where they were gassed or killed by disease, maltreatment, or ghoulish scientific "experiments." Estimating the total number of Roma victims of the Nazis is very difficult, but it was at least in the hundreds of thousands.

Nazi policies were the epitome of racially motivated murder, but ethnic hatreds fuelled many other atrocities. In various parts of Central and Eastern Europe the ambitions of various nationalists, and the conviction that some ethnic groups were inherently traitorous, led to waves of killing. In the occupied Yugoslav lands, for instance, the Axis satellite state of Croatia soon embarked upon a campaign of racial "purification." Ante Pavelić, leader of the fascist Ustaša, who had been installed as the Paglovnik (ruler) of Croatia, oversaw the murder of 50,000 Jews and 250,000 Serbs. In addition, hundreds of thousands of Serbs were either deported or forced to convert to Catholicism. To the south, where the former Yugoslav province of Kosovo had been transferred to Italian-controlled Albania, previous Serb domination was challenged by the local Albanian majority, producing a spiral of violence. An Italian observer described how "Slavs and Albanians had burned down one another's houses, had killed as many people as possible, and had stolen livestock, goods, and tools."[10]

As the quotation suggests, civilians could be perpetrators as well as victims in this war-torn region, and the violence between ethnic groups was often mutual and reinforcing. Serbs, including members of the Chetnik resistance movement, engaged in attacks upon Croats and Bosnian Muslims, whom Serb ultra-nationalists accused of being allies of the Ustaša. Some Bosnian Muslims were, but others joined the Communist Partisans, and some even cooperated with the Chetniks on occasion. The patterns of ethnic violence in wartime Yugoslavia were thus both incredibly complex and immensely destructive. The majority of the 1.2 million Yugoslavs killed in the war died at the hands of fellow citizens.

Conflict between Ukrainians and Poles was also widespread. Before the war a substantial number of Ukrainians had lived under a Polish regime that they considered, with some justification, as prejudicial. During the war radical nationalists saw the opportunity to establish an independent state, believing they would have to cleanse "their" territory of Poles to do so. For their part, some Polish nationalists, who wanted to rebuild their country after the war, believed that the Ukrainian minority could not be trusted and had to be "removed." Beginning in 1943, towns and villages where Poles and Ukrainians had sometimes peacefully coexisted for decades were rent by communal violence in which tens of thousands died. Waldemar Lotnik, who fought on the Polish side in this conflict, joined the killing after his uncles were murdered by Ukrainian nationalists in December 1943. He and a group of comrades avenged Polish losses by killing 16 Ukrainians, one of them an eight-year-old boy. Though that particular killing was accidental, at the time Lotnik "felt no remorse for my part in what happened: this was war and revenge at last."[11] The hatreds unleashed by such violence echoed into the postwar era, notwithstanding later, often brutal efforts by the Soviets to impose order.

The Soviet Union engaged in a variety of forced population removals. Early in the war, Stalin capitalized upon his agreement with Hitler to gain control over Poland's eastern territories in 1939, the Baltic States in 1940, and northern Bukovina and Bessarabia, which were annexed from Romania that same year. For the Soviet dictator consolidating a Communist presence meant getting rid of political opponents and those from potentially troublesome occupations and social classes: army officers, police, educators, civil servants, and some wealthy businesspeople and farmers. By 1941 2 million families had been expelled from Poland alone to Central Asia and Siberia; thousands died on the journey or during their internment. Following the Nazi invasion of June 1941 entire nationalities, whom Stalin deemed to be potential traitors, were rounded up; for instance, 948,000 Soviet ethnic Germans were sent east to labour camps or remote "special settlements." Later in the war, as the Red Army started to drive the *Wehrmacht* from its territory, entire nationalities were deported because some individuals had collaborated with the Germans. Among the groups forcibly removed from their homes were the Chechens, Kalmyks, and Crimean Tatars. Roughly one-quarter of these deportees perished in the first years of exile.

Aerial Bombardment and Civilian Deaths

During the interwar years military planners and politicians had been intensely concerned about the impact of aerial attacks upon civilians. Hints of what could happen appeared during the First World War, and subsequent events such as Fascist Italy's bombardment of Ethiopia and deaths due to air attacks in the Spanish Civil War reinforced the notion that air raids would cause massive destruction and death, leading to social breakdown and the collapse of popular morale. During the Second World War aerial attacks intended to crush morale were conducted on a massive scale, yet the bomber often proved unable to break the resolve of enemy populations, even though bombing campaigns were immensely destructive and had terrible social and psychological consequences.

The use of air power against civilians during the war was pervasive. Japan's assault upon China was supported by repeated air attacks on cities such as Shanghai and Nanjing; later, Japanese bombers repeatedly struck the wartime Nationalist capital of Chonqing. Air raids may have killed up to 300,000 Chinese non-combatants between 1931 and 1945. The *Luftwaffe* (German air force) also systematically bombed civilians. Warsaw was heavily targeted during the September 1939 invasion. When the Germans attacked in the spring of 1940 they bombed the Dutch city of Rotterdam, killing nearly 900 people and rendering some 78,500 homeless; this event helped to trigger a massive refugee crisis. In the late summer of 1940, after failing to destroy the RAF and invade Britain, the Reich conducted a protracted terror bombing campaign against British cities. When the Nazi war machine moved east in 1941, it was the turn of Belgrade, Athens, and other such cities to suffer; the Yugoslav capital alone may have lost between 5,000 and 10,000 of its citizens. German aircraft also carried out countless raids in connection with Operation Barbarossa and later offensives in the Soviet Union, destroying villages and towns, and wreaking havoc upon cities such as Leningrad, Moscow, and Stalingrad, killing an estimated 40,000 civilians in the latter city alone.

The British-controlled island of Malta provides another arresting example of the sustained bombing of civilians. Of critical importance as a base for air and sea operations against the Axis in the Mediterranean, it came under repeated air attack from the Italians and Germans. The raids were extraordinarily intense during the first half of 1942; from 1 January to 24 July of that year there was only one 24-hour period when bombs did not fall on the island. Nearly 1,500 Maltese were killed and over 3,700 injured (out of a total population of 270,000) by bombing; during its worst phase they essentially lived underground, suffering from malnutrition and disease. But the battered populace held on until the Axis defeat in North Africa in 1943.

The German aerial assault on Britain, the Allied bomber offensive against Nazi Germany, and US raids on Japan are the bombing campaigns that have been most thoroughly analyzed. The first of these is typically associated with the daylight raids against British cities, which began in the summer of 1940 in preparation for an invasion that never came. After inflicting considerable damage but also suffering substantial losses, the Germans postponed Operation Sea Lion indefinitely, but the *Luftwaffe* continued to strike British cities, increasingly at night. London endured 76 nights of consecutive attacks (with one exception, 2 November) between 7 September 1940 and 10 May 1941. During this same period the *Luftwaffe* also struck over 100 cities, towns, and villages throughout England, Scotland, and Wales, as well as Belfast in Northern Ireland. Over 43,000 people were killed during this period, and an even greater number were seriously injured; casualties among air raid wardens and firefighters were especially high. Beyond these losses, some 2.25 million Britons were made homeless.

Given the circumstances, the authorities were concerned that the social fabric of the country might unravel. Reflecting the class suspicions common among many members of the British elite, they were particularly concerned that members of the working class would break down. There were indeed signs of strain; people tended to become critical of the authorities in cases where anti-aircraft fire was lacking, when adequate shelter was not available, or when either the response time or size of the emergency services proved inadequate. Geoffrey Hill, a 15-year-old from Sheffield, recalled the scene after a German attack: "On street corners there were stretchers with bodies on them covered in tarpaulin waiting to be moved ... for weeks water wagons had to supply people [and there were] no toilets or electricity."[12] The British Home Office reported discontent in London because its working-class districts were being hit more often; reports of Britons expressing anti-Semitic views also increased. Nor were elements of the population—including some air raid wardens and firefighters—above looting property.

Yet morale held. Though there were some tragic errors and shortcomings, the authorities improved emergency responses, built more shelters, and refined warning systems and defences. Most of the population adapted as well as they could, adjusting their routines as necessary and hoping for the best; some even reported a sense of excitement and purpose in the face of danger, while others found their hatred for Germany intensified. The authorities encouraged stoicism and confidence; many people embraced or at least complied with these messages, even though their bodies could betray signs of stress—hair falling out, panic attacks, and increased stomach disorders and ulcers. Eric Sevareid, a US foreign correspondent based in London at the time, captured the strain of experiencing intense fear and trying to carry on:

> The people of Britain were brave and heroic in their endurance during those frightful weeks.... But it would be to make them more than human and thus to do them less than justice to suggest that none at any time betrayed stark fear or that there were no individual cases of panic and hysteria.... The British may not be a hot-blooded or excitable people, but they are still people.... The day the Germans raided the docks, the first great daylight raid on London ... I saw terror in the eyes of hundreds as they moved in a great migration away from the awesome pillars of black oil smoke, trudging through snowpiles of powdered glass, pushing their prams, heads turned over shoulders, staring eyes fixed upon the quiet and mocking sky.[13]

After May 1941 the raids abated, though German bombers returned in 1942 and again in early 1944. Even after the Allies had landed in Normandy in June 1944, Britons still had to fear death from the air, as German V-1 "flying bombs" and V-2 rockets were launched at them. They remained a threat until March 1945, killing 8,618 people, injuring thousands more, and causing vast property damage. Coming at a time when victory seemed both certain and yet frustratingly elusive, and following years of privation, it is not surprising that these new weapons had an adverse effect on morale; they were both frighteningly unfamiliar and difficult to defend against, in particular the supersonic V-2. But the V-weapons had the psychological impact they did partly because the British people had already endured the more serious threat of 1940–41, when the future of their state hung in the balance. In 1944–45 such fortitude seemed less necessary.

By that time Nazi Germany was demanding its citizens show ever more discipline in response to bombardment, but it was very difficult for them to do so. German cities—including Berlin and above all Hamburg—had been attacked since 1940, and from 1942 onwards British Commonwealth and US air crews mounted a systematic campaign. The United States Army Air Force (USAAF) concentrated on daytime, precision, strategic bombing, though in practice it hit civilian targets. RAF Bomber Command dedicated itself to night-time "area bombing"; the aim was to destroy not only infrastructure but also civilian housing and morale. In the early stages of the offensive, casualties due to German anti-aircraft fire and fighters were almost prohibitively high, but the Allies persisted and the introduction of fighter escorts reduced, though it never eliminated, the risk to bomber crews. Huge fleets of aircraft, sometimes numbering over 1,000 bombers, ranged across the skies of Germany and occupied Europe. A wave of attacks on Hamburg in July–August 1943 caused firestorms in that city, killing 40,000 people, seriously injuring 125,000, and leaving some 900,000 homeless; a series of raids on Berlin in the winter of 1943–44 left 9,000 dead.

The bombing intensified in 1944 and 1945, continuing to strike not only industrial and urban targets but also transport and oil reserves. The death toll mounted. While Allied aircrews paid a high price, some 80,000 men in total, losses in Germany accelerated, from approximately 100,000 over the course of 1943 to 200,000 in 1944, with an additional 50,000 to 100,000 people being killed from January 1945 to the time of the Reich's final surrender. One of the most destructive, and controversial, attacks of the final stages of the war was the series of raids staged on the city of Dresden in February 1945, which killed at least 35,000 people. In total, between 400,000 to 500,000 people were killed in the raids on Germany; 10 per cent of them were POWs and foreign labourers.

Initially the population of the Third Reich seemed to withstand the onslaught, but whereas in Britain the scale of attacks lessened over time, and the V-weapon strikes came when victory seemed likely, in the case of Germany the bombing became ever more destructive and coincided with news of growing military reverses. By 1943 the strain was clearly beginning to show. The devastation of Hamburg, for example, was followed by a chaotic mass flight from the city. In some cases people wearing Nazi Party badges had them ripped from their coats and were threatened, as those associated with the regime were now blamed for bringing terror upon Germany. In Nuremberg, the home of Nazi rallies but also the target of repeated bombing attacks, the authorities noted that the raids had resulted in a growing obsession with security and a narrowing of people's horizons to concentrate on their personal well-being and that of their families. As one official put it, "mentally the constant threat from the air is having an ever-more damaging effect. Broad sectors of the population sit around the wireless until midnight, using electricity and heating unnecessarily."[14] Young children who could not yet fully grasp what was going on quickly learned fear from adults. A resident of the city of Essen recalled, "I was born at the outbreak of the war so that I cannot remember the first years. But from my fifth year on, much is ineradicably etched in my memory, I sat through long nights of bombing in the cellar or bunker between shaking adults."[15]

The Third Reich responded by expanding defences, paying compensation to victims, and evacuating some 8 million people, primarily from urban to more rural areas. Propaganda Minister Josef Goebbels also sought to channel popular anger towards not only the Allies but also "International Jewry," whom he suggested were ultimately responsible for Germany's woes. Popular anger towards foreigners certainly increased. In addition to some instances of downed Allied aircrew being lynched, foreign workers sometimes also became targets; one 14-year-old Polish domestic servant, living with a German family near Danzig, recalled how she was beaten by her mistress every time Berlin was bombed, because the latter's husband worked in the capital.[16] But while elements of the German populace shared the regime's racist outlook, this did not always benefit morale. One Hamburg resident recalled that during the 1943 raids, "In private and even in bigger circles, simple people, the middle classes and the rest of the population make repeated remarks about the Allied attacks being the revenge for our treatment of the Jews."[17] Here was a case of people accepting Goebbels's postulate that Jews directed the Allied war effort, but also blaming their government for what had befallen them.

As the war neared its end, many of Germany's cities were in a process of social disintegration. Nearly three-quarters of the housing in Hamburg and Cologne was destroyed; some communities were rendered uninhabitable. The Nazi regime's attempts to provide shelter and aid had raised its profile for a time, but its efforts were gradually overwhelmed. Aid workers, for instance, were bombed out of their residences, and while many rural districts had at first welcomed evacuees, there were also regional and social tensions, comparable to but more intense than those experienced in Britain. Also in contrast to Britain, the Nazi regime increasingly resorted to repression in order to maintain control. Significant looting during or after air raids was punished by the death penalty. Though it was ultimately invading armies and not the bombing campaign on its own that ended the Third Reich, it seems clear that bombing had done much to cause social dislocation and growing pessimism, even despair. By the winter of 1945 parents in Nuremberg opposed the evacuation of their children to smaller centres, as they feared these places would also be attacked. As one local official reported, "The response now is 'we want to die with our children.'"[18]

Though the bulk of their efforts were devoted to the Reich itself, the Allies also hit targets in Italy and throughout occupied Europe. Allied air raids killed approximately 64,000 Italians over the course of the war, disrupted industrial production, and had considerable psychological impact. Italians quickly directed their anger towards Mussolini's regime for bringing them into war and responding inadequately to bombings. One resident of Porto Empedocle in Sicily encapsulated the growing disaffection: "there was no alarm—it's always like this—it's torture—here, everyone has run off to the countryside or sleeps in the shelters—it's a terrible life in the shelters, it's filthy—full of lice—of mange—of illness—a disgrace."[19] With respect to occupied France, Belgium, and the Netherlands, Allied planners tended to be circumspect in choosing targets, concerned about the political implications of civilian casualties. But strategic priorities and the escalating dynamic of war meant tens of thousands of deaths in spite of these considerations, approximately 60,000 in France alone. In instances where the purpose of British or US bombing was unclear, or the level of destruction was seen as disproportionate—such as a raid on Le Havre in 1944—there could be incomprehension, even anger, on the part of the locals. But the evidence also suggests that if the latter perceived that a target had obvious strategic importance for the Allies, they could display considerable patience.

The USAAF was not in a position to conduct a systematic bombing campaign against Japan until late in the war, though it had struck Tokyo as early as April 1942, and there were also sorties flown from China until a Japanese offensive in 1944 overran the bases. Following the capture of Saipan, however, the Americans could send regular B-29 raids against the Japanese home islands from November 1944 onwards. Initially they concentrated upon precision strikes on strategic targets but then shifted their efforts to the destruction of civilian housing and morale. Japanese urban dwellings were concentrated in small areas and often constructed of highly flammable materials; this meant that incendiary bombings in particular caused immense destruction. Beginning with a huge attack on Tokyo on the night of 9/10 March 1945, US bombers undertook a series of raids that devastated Japan's major cities within a matter of a few months. The first Tokyo attack, which lasted for two and a half hours, caused fires that burned for as long as four days. The raid likely killed 90,000 people and possibly more. Alongside those consumed by flames many perished as a result of suffocation, as the fires consumed their oxygen; others drowned as they tried to escape by jumping into the Onagigawa River. Additional deaths followed the actual bombings. Funato Kazuyo and her sister Hiroko survived the attack, but Hiroko's hands were badly burned; her sister placed them in the moist soil of an air raid shelter to soothe them, but as a result Hiroko contracted tetanus and died.[20]

In the weeks that followed there were additional strikes on the Japanese capital, as well as on cities such as Nagoya, Osaka, and Kobe; eventually the USAAF began to announce its targets in advance, impressing upon the Japanese the extent to which they were defenceless. Though casualty figures remain an issue of contention, the US Strategic Bombing Survey estimated 330,000 deaths due to bombing, including some Allied POWs and foreign residents; 476,000 people were seriously injured, and 2.5 million buildings were destroyed; over 8 million people fled their homes. In terms of civilian morale responses to the air raids were complex. Air raid drills and relief work continued; people seemed to cope better if they could play an active role, even as a member of a bucket brigade dousing fires. The fact that Japanese living standards had been falling for some time reduced the opportunities for the kinds of theft that had taken place in bombed-out Britain and Germany. After Yokohama was hit on 29 May 1945, for instance, one observer noted that looting was not a major problem, as there was little to steal.[21]

While the bombing may not have brought about total collapse, it was profoundly disruptive. With millions left homeless and/or relocated to rural areas, traditional patterns of work and life vanished. A report to the

Imperial Cabinet in June 1945 indicated that public attitudes towards the government and the military were souring. As in Germany, some complained that it was the government's fault that the Japanese people were suffering. One 18-year-old wrote in her diary on 21 July 1945 that "Everything considered I wish I had ended up dying during the bombings. If only there weren't a war, we wouldn't have to pretend we were happy."[22]

The Final Stages

In the end the Axis states were decisively defeated. In 1943 Fascist Italy became the first regime to fall, but this hardly ended the tribulations of the Italian people. Following the Allied landings on Sicily on 10 July, King Victor Emmanuel III dismissed Mussolini and had him arrested. He appointed a new prime minister, Marshal Pietro Badoglio, who began talks with the Allies, but in the meantime the Germans poured additional troops into Italy. The Allies landed on the Italian mainland on 8 September 1943, but the expanded German forces mounted a fierce resistance, while Badoglio and the king fled south to safety under Allied protection. The Germans freed Mussolini and installed him as the ruler of a puppet regime, the Italian Social Republic (RSI), based in the northern town of Salò. Thus, from the fall of 1943 until the spring of 1945, Italy was the scene not only of a bitter struggle between a multinational Allied force and the Germans but also an internecine conflict between an expanding Italian resistance movement and the supporters of the RSI.

Italians soon discovered that being liberated could be dangerous, even deadly. Air strikes continued; artillery fire and troop movements forced evacuations, making tens of thousands of people refugees in their own country. Reactions to the Allied presence partly depended upon circumstances. In Naples, where there had been a costly uprising against the German occupiers, Allied troops were popular partly because once the city was liberated their spending did a great deal to revive the local economy. Even though there were instances of violence, and prostitution was widespread, one visiting Italian official remarked in 1945 that "what people fear most is the end of the war."[23] By contrast Rome, which was liberated in June 1944, seemed less hospitable. Though it had been declared an open city and had avoided major destruction, its economy declined and did not benefit from the Allied presence. Whatever resentment the Allies created, however, paled in comparison to the anger roused by the brutal German presence in central and northern Italy. Into the autumn of 1944 thousands of Italians were rounded up to work for the Reich. Retreating German troops also laid waste to infrastructure, creating immense challenges for reconstruction.

Under these conditions in northern Italy partisan groups of various political stripes—the largest of them the Communists—gained strength, reaching a membership of perhaps 250,000 by the spring of 1945. As for Mussolini's Salò Republic, it could not be described as popular but was able to draw upon some reserves of support from younger generations as well as long-time Fascists. This meant that northern Italy was wracked by what was in effect a civil war, which proved very dangerous for the often ill-equipped partisans; some 45,000 lost their lives. The Germans and their RSI allies also took and shot hostages. One of the most infamous of these incidents was the murder of 335 civilians at the Ardeatine Caves outside Rome in March 1944 in response to a partisan attack that had killed 33 soldiers. The growing fury of the partisans was such that they did not shrink from shooting Fascist supporters outright, their most famous victims being Mussolini and his mistress, captured in April 1945.

Following the D-Day landings on 6 June 1944 similar patterns unfolded in Western Europe. Resistance operations could have unintended but deadly consequences. The most notorious German reprisal in France was the murder of 642 people in the village of Oradour-sur-Glâne on 8 June 1944, by troops from the SS Panzer Das Reich Division, some of whom were conscripted Alsatians, on their way to fight in Normandy. Oradour was not a major centre of resistance, but it was suspected of having an arms cache. When the inhabitants failed to produce any arms, the men were rounded up and shot, while women and children were barricaded in a local church that was then set ablaze.

The fighting in Normandy following the landings proved lethal for non-combatants as well as the opposing armies. The landscape was deeply scarred, and some towns and cities, notably Caen and Saint-Lô, were levelled. It is likely that one-third of the French civilians killed by Allied bombing—some 20,000 people—died in Normandy during this period. Thus, while local populations were aware that they were being liberated, especially in areas of intense fighting, their attitude towards US, British, and Canadian troops was not always enthusiastic. Major Edward Elliott of the Glasgow Highlanders grasped why, commenting: "the French are having a pretty thin time at present. First the Germans dig holes all over the place and pull down houses, then we shell and bomb their homes and drive [our] vehicles all over the fields. Naturally their attitude towards us is inclined to be a bit stiff; however, I think they are mostly for us, though they are desperately tired of the war and the misery it has caused them."[24]

Outside of the areas of most intense combat the reception seemed more enthusiastic. Parisians experienced fighting when the French resistance rose up against the Germans in August 1944 but not the devastation that occurred in Normandy. The Belgians, too, greeted their liberators warmly, but faced renewed misery during the last, desperate German attempt to stem the Allied advance, the Battle of the Bulge of December 1944–January 1945. Though the Nazi counterattack was eventually defeated, lives were lost as "collateral damage" to Allied air strikes and to atrocities carried out by German troops, who also killed US prisoners at Malmédy. In addition, the cities of Liège and Antwerp suffered repeated V-weapon attacks. For the Dutch the last winter of the war was the most difficult. Though about one-fifth of Holland was liberated by September 1944, and Canadian troops fought doggedly to free the rest of the country, the German decision to punish the Dutch for striking in support of Allied efforts by cutting off all food imports resulted in about 16,000 people starving to death during "the Hunger Winter." When the country was completely liberated in May 1945, the Dutch population gave the Canadians an enthusiastic welcome, but malnutrition remained a serious problem. First Canadian Army reported between 100,000 and 150,000 cases of starvation edema in western Holland, with a death rate of 10 per cent; those over 60 were especially susceptible.

Earlier in that cruel winter the Western Allies had crossed the frontier into Germany. Even though all hope of victory was gone, the leaders of the Third Reich ordered resistance to the bitter end. The result, Richard Bessel comments, was that "Germany in January 1945 became the site of what perhaps was the greatest killing frenzy the world has ever seen."[25] One-quarter of the Reich's military losses during the entire war, totalling some 1.3 million deaths, occurred in the last four months of fighting. German civilians were now constantly in the line of fire. The Nazi leaders resorted to threats and force to stiffen resolve. In March 1945 Hitler decreed the destruction of anything that could be of use to the invaders and the arrest of relatives of soldiers who surrendered without fighting. On 3 April Himmler ordered that if a house flew a white flag, all of the male inhabitants should be shot. Such commands speak not only to the fanaticism of the regime but also to the fact that the will to fight, especially against the British and Americans, was beginning to crumble. Some German units went on to the end, sometimes with the support of members of the *Volkssturm*, an auxiliary militia created in the autumn of 1944 composed of males aged 16 to 60. In fact, boys younger than age 16 had also gone into action against the Allies as members of the Hitler Youth. In the final weeks of fighting desertion rates rose, and some *Volkssturm* units, ill-equipped and facing hopeless odds, simply gave up.

In a growing number of cases civilians were surrendering their communities. Sometimes this objective was eased by the fact that the local Nazi officials fled, but those who stuck to their posts could turn ferociously on dissenters. The town of Oschenfurt, in the region of Franconia, is illustrative. Local women began to dismantle tank obstacles, even driving off a few members of the *Volkssturm* in the process, while a delegation demanded that the local Nazi party boss surrender to the Americans. He refused, arresting three of the women and sentencing them to hang; fortunately US troops arrived before the executions could be carried out.

Harsh as conditions were in the West, the scale of destruction was even greater in the East. Resistance movements suffered terribly. The largest of these uprisings was the attempt by the Polish Home Army, beginning on 1 August 1944, to seize control of Warsaw before the Red Army arrived, in the hope of forestalling what they feared would be total Soviet control. Instead, the Red Army halted and the insurgents were crushed by the Germans, with as many as 200,000 Poles losing their lives as their capital was reduced to rubble. In neighbouring Slovakia, where public opinion was turning against the collaborationist regime of Monsignor Josef Tiso, a mass uprising by dissident military and partisan forces seized control of some central districts of the country in August and September of the same year, but the Germans crushed this rebellion as well; some 25,000 Slovaks perished.

Ferocious as the Germans were in dealing with resisters, they were still being pushed back by the Red Army, many of whose soldiers behaved with great brutality as they moved into enemy territory. Hardened by years of intense fighting and German depredations, their hatred and desire for revenge was reinforced by propaganda, with often terrifying results for German troops and civilians. The capture of the East Prussian village of Nemmersdorf in October 1944 by Red Army troops provided an early sign of what was to come. After the *Wehrmacht* briefly re-took the village, it reported that numerous civilians—men, women, and children—had been killed in the most gruesome manner. Nazi propaganda used the incident to steel civilian and military resolve against the Soviets. To a degree this appears to have worked, for intense fighting continued in the East until the bitter end. The city of Breslau, for example, was besieged from February until early May 1945. The Red Army also paid a high price in taking Berlin, in a battle that lasted from 16 April to 2 May. In addition to the lives lost in the fighting, Soviet troops terrorized the surviving civilians, engaged in looting, killing, and rape. Sexual assault was a problem during the liberation of Western Europe as well, with hundreds of US, British, and French soldiers being charged with rape. However, what unfolded in the East took place on a much larger scale. An estimated 1.4 million women in eastern Germany, ranging from children to the elderly, were assaulted during this period, 100,000 of them in Berlin alone. Many women were attacked more than once, by gangs and often in public in order to terrorize them and humiliate their male relatives, who were often killed if they tried to interfere.

Thousands of Germans took their own lives during these months; suicides accounted for approximately 3,000 of the 10,000 civilians who died during the siege of Breslau. In some cases family members—most often fathers—killed their spouses and children rather than see them fall into the hands of the Soviets or live in a defeated Germany. Those who wanted to live took flight; at least 7 million people from eastern Germany became refugees during the winter of 1945. Some evacuations ended in tragedy: the *Wilhelm Gustloff*, which had been a liner for the Nazi "Strength through Joy" leisure and touring organization, was carrying 6,600 refugees through the Baltic when it was torpedoed by a Soviet submarine; 5,300 of those aboard perished.

It must be noted that at this time some 700,000 surviving inmates of camps located in the East, the majority of them Jews, were being forcibly relocated to camps within Germany itself. Approximately 250,000 of them were killed if they could not keep up on forced marches or were simply shot out of hand. Thus, before Hitler's short-lived successor, Admiral Karl Dönitz, finally surrendered on 8 May 1945, the remnants of the Nazi state had both compelled its people to endure a paroxysm of violence, and pursued its murderous racial agenda to the very end.

The Japanese empire's determination to fight on even after it was clear the war was lost also had terrible consequences. From the summer of 1944 on the Allies were evidently closing in. In New Guinea, US and Australian troops made steady if difficult progress. In the central Pacific US forces took key islands in the Marianas. The Americans also devoted major forces to the liberation of the Philippines, landing on the key island of Luzon in January 1945 and regaining control of Manila by March, after heavy fighting. In the spring and summer of 1945 US forces took the key islands of Iwo Jima and Okinawa, despite fierce Japanese resistance. By this time British imperial forces were also inflicting significant defeats upon the Japanese army in Southeast Asia; after thwarting a Japanese offensive into northeast India they invaded Burma in December 1944 and retook the capital of Rangoon in May 1945.

Preparations were made for an invasion of the Japanese home islands themselves in the winter of 1945–46, something Allied planners anticipated would be a costly undertaking. These plans were rendered unnecessary by the US decision to drop atomic bombs, first on Hiroshima and then Nagasaki, on 6 and 9 August 1945 respectively. On 8 August the Japanese were also dismayed to learn that the Soviets, in keeping with a commitment made to the British and Americans, had declared war. The Red Army moved swiftly into Japanese-controlled Manchuria, inflicting significant casualties before the Emperor of Japan finally announced an unconditional surrender on 15 August. In some areas Japanese troops continued to fight for several days, only giving up after they were directly ordered to stand down; indeed, a few Japanese soldiers continued to hide out on Pacific islands for decades after the war ended.

From the civilian perspective there were significant parallels between experiences in Asia and Europe during the last stages of the war. Many of those being freed from Japanese rule were caught in the crossfire of opposing forces and the vengeance of withdrawing Japanese soldiers. Nowhere was this more evident than in the capital of the Philippines between February and March 1945. Japanese commanders decided to fight the Americans for control of the city, which led to the extensive use of US artillery. This caused civilian deaths; the residents were also frequently attacked by Japanese troops on the grounds that anyone left in the battle zone was supposedly a guerrilla. What had become an all-too-familiar cycle of pillage, rape, and mass shootings recurred; among the massacre sites were schools, hospitals, and convents. Juan Labrador, a priest who taught at Manila's Santo Tomas University before the Japanese occupation, commented on the atrocities during the battle: "The accounts are so terrifying and macabre that my spirit was filled with infinite bitterness, and I wept with tears of pain and indignation. From this sadness and sympathy arose an impotent anger against the infernal forces which vented its desperation and hate among the civilian populace. So many families of acquaintances and friends exterminated. So many mutilated."[26] As many as 100,000 civilians were killed during the struggle for Manila. By contrast, Burma's capital of Rangoon was not fought over, but Japanese troops wrought havoc before withdrawing. When British imperial forces entered the city in March 1945, there was no public transport, electricity, or sanitation services operating, and some quarters of the city had also been devastated by Allied bombing.

As we have seen, in Europe liberating Allied soldiers were frequently welcomed with open arms, but on occasion local enthusiasm was tempered by loss of life and property and sometimes by the actions of the soldiers themselves. The situation was perhaps even more complex in Asia. To be sure, there were many scenes of joy: the devastation of Manila did not prevent many Filipinos and Filipinas from welcoming US troops. But in other cases, the situation was different. In Manchuria, some Chinese civilians were sexually assaulted by Red Army troops who were "liberating" them from Japanese rule. Moreover, Allied victories were often followed by attempts to restore imperial rule. Many Asians were glad to see Japan defeated, but they did not want the return of colonialism. As we have seen, in some cases—notably with Sukarno in Indonesia and Ho Chi Minh in Vietnam—local anti-colonialists tried to assert independence amidst the Japanese collapse.

For the Japanese people the last months of the war were agonizing. A highly successful US submarine offensive left their economy on life support, and major cities were devastated by bombing. But a still-fearsome state apparatus, devotion to the regime, and fear of the Allies meant that many people continued to support the war effort and were unable to accept defeat. The use of kamikazes and the suicide of large numbers of Japanese soldiers are both well-known, but, as in Nazi Germany, large numbers of civilians also killed themselves during the final desperate months of the conflict. When it became clear during the summer of 1944 that the armed forces would not be able to hold Saipan, hundreds of Japanese settlers ended their own lives, some by jumping from cliffs. Between 30,000 and 100,000 residents of Okinawa perished as Japanese and US troops battled for control of the island; some were killed by US troops, others by Japanese soldiers, but a significant proportion of the deaths were suicides. The evidence suggests that carnage on an even greater scale might have occurred if the Japanese home islands had been invaded. Morale was clearly waning, but most dissent remained private, and the imperial government took desperate measures, including the formation of civilian militia units, armed with bamboo spears or even awls, in an effort to prepare for Allied landings.

It never came to that. Instead, some 80,000 residents of Hiroshima and at least 40,000 residents of Nagasaki—Japanese civilians, Korean labourers, and some Allied POWs—perished in the atomic bombings; tens of thousands more died from radiation sickness or other injuries in the weeks, months, and years that followed. Survivors were afflicted in a multitude of ways. Fumiko Morishita was a waitress in Hiroshima when the bomb hit; she was not immediately injured but was soon stricken with radiation poisoning. She refused to marry her soldier fiancé because she witnessed the impact of radiation on newborns and did not wish to see the same thing happen to their children. Despite his insistence that he still wanted to marry her, she refused.[27] Historians continue to debate whether the dropping of the bombs was necessary and whether it was the bombings themselves that led Japan's leaders to finally surrender. Whatever the case, it seems clear that the latter decision was greeted with mixed feelings by many Japanese, as illustrated by the comments of Ichiro Hatano, a teenager: "The war is over. Yet, despite my feelings of relief, I cannot welcome the news whole-heartedly. I hate the idea of our unconditional surrender; to my mind death would have been preferable."[28]

Conclusion

The Second World War shattered the lives of civilians on an unprecedented scale, both in terms of the numbers of people involved and in the intensity of death and destruction. The targeting of civilians, whether by invading armies on the ground or through aerial bombardment, could and sometimes did lead to panic, collapse, or sometimes a gradual erosion of commitment to the war effort. Many civilians also contributed to the violence. Though many of the campaigns of genocide and ethnic cleansing during the war were initiated by states, past hatreds, opportunism, and political choice led ordinary people to turn on or even help purge their neighbours and to acquiesce in and sometimes promote the persecution of minorities.

Wartime violence could destroy lives even when it did not end them and led to lasting trauma and despair, sometimes to the point of suicide. But it could also strengthen the will to resist. Various civilian populations withstood intense bombing for periods of time that would have surprised many commentators in the 1920s and 1930s. Resisters and minorities increasingly fought back, even though the chances of prevailing against professional armies were often slim. For those who came through the violence, a variety of political and emotional responses beckoned. The desire for justice, for revenge, and for toppling of old structures was often strong. But also powerful was the desire to have done with the violence and rebuild, to seek order and security, and even to forget what had happened. These complex, and often coexisting impulses, played out in various ways following the German and Japanese surrenders.

Further Reading

On invading armies in Asia, Werner Gruhl, *Imperial Japan's World War Two 1931–1945* (New Brunswick, NJ: Transaction Publishers, 2007) provides much information. Iris Chang's *The Rape of Nanking: The Forgotten Holocaust of World War II* (New York: BasicBooks, 1997) drew renewed attention to the massacre, but see also the essays in Bob Tadashi Wakabayashi, ed., *The Nanking Atrocity, 1937–38: Complicating the Picture* (New York: Berghahn Books, 2007). For the German army in 1939 see Alexander Rossino, *Hitler Strikes Poland: Blitzkrieg, Ideology, and Atrocity* (Lawrence, KS: University Press of Kansas, 2003). Hannah Diamond, *Fleeing Hitler: France 1940* (Oxford: Oxford University Press, 2007) conveys the experience of the "exodus."

In addition to the studies of the Holocaust cited in Chapter 2, see also Joshua Rubenstein and Ilya Altman, eds., *The Unknown Black Book: The Holocaust in the German-Occupied Soviet Territories* (Bloomington, IN: Indiana State University Press, 2008); Father Patrick Desbois, *The Holocaust by Bullets: A Priest's Journey to Uncover the Truth behind the Murder of 1.5 Million Jews* (New York: Palgrave Macmillan, 2008); Yitzhak Arad, *Belzec, Sobibor, Treblinka: The Operation Reinhard Death Camps* (Bloomington, IN: Indiana State University Press, 1987); and Yisrael Gutman and Michael Berenbaum, eds., *Anatomy of the Auschwitz Death Camp* (Bloomington, IN: Indiana State University Press, 1994). On other Nazi victims, see Suzanne Evans, *Forgotten Crimes: The Holocaust and People with Disabilities* (Chicago, IL: Ivan R. Dee, 2004) and Gunter Lewy, *The Nazi Persecution of the Gypsies* (New York: Oxford University Press, 2000). On the ethnic conflicts in Yugoslavia and the Soviet Union, see Benjamin Lieberman, *Terrible Fate: Ethnic Cleansing in the Making of Modern Europe* (Chicago, IL: Ivan R. Dee, 2006).

Regarding air attacks on British civilians, recent accounts include Peter Stansky, *The First Day of the Blitz: September 7, 1940* (New Haven, CT: Yale University Press, 2007) and Amy Bell, "Landscapes of Fear: Wartime London, 1939–1945," *Journal of British Studies* 48:1 (2009): 153–75. For Germany, see Jörg Friedrich, *The Fire: The Bombing of Germany, 1940–1945* (New York: Columbia University Press, 2006), though some of his arguments are controversial. See also Nicholas Stargardt, *Witnesses of War: Children's Lives under the Nazis* (London: Jonathan Cape, 2005) and Neil Gregor, "A *Schicksalsgemeinshaft?* Allied Bombing, Civilian Morale, and Social Dissolution in Nuremberg, 1942–1945," *Historical Journal* 43:4 (2000): 1051–70. On Japan, see Kenneth Werrell, *Blankets of Fire: US Bombers over Japan during World War II* (Washington, DC: Smithsonian Institution Press, 1992) and Haruko Taya Cook and Theodore F. Cook, eds., *Japan at War: An Oral History* (New York: The New Press, 1992).

On the closing stages of the war in Europe, see William Hitchcock, *The Bitter Road to Freedom: A New History of the Liberation of Europe* (New York: Free Press, 2008); Richard Bessel, *Germany 1945: From War to Peace* (New York:

HarperCollins, 2009); and Stephen Fritz, *Endkampf: Soldiers, Civilians, and the Death of the Third Reich* (Lexington, KY: University Press of Kentucky, 2004). On the issue of rape, see Jeffrey Burds, "Sexual Violence in Europe in World War II, 1939–1945," *Politics & Society* 37:1 (2009): 35–74. On the final stages of the Pacific War, see Richard Frank, *Downfall: The End of the Imperial Japanese Empire* (New York: Random House, 1999). Max Hastings, *Armageddon: The Battle for Germany, 1944–45* (New York: Random House, 2004) and *Nemesis: The Battle for Japan, 1944–45* (London: Harper Press, 2007) recount the final stages of the European and Asian wars in detail.

Notes

1   Quoted in Werner Gruhl, *Imperial Japan's World War Two 1931–1945* (New Brunswick, NJ: Transaction Publishers, 2007), 78.
2   Quoted in Alexander Rossino, *Hitler Strikes Poland: Blitzkrieg, Ideology, and Atrocity* (Lawrence, KS: University Press of Kansas, 2003), 139.
3   Quoted in Evans, *The Third Reich at War*, 198.
4   Quoted in Harrison Salisbury, *The 900 Days: The Siege of Leningrad* (New York: Harper and Row, 1969), 441.
5   Quoted in Hannah Diamond, *Fleeing Hitler: France 1940* (Oxford: Oxford University Press, 2007), 71.
6   Quoted in Joshua Rubenstein and Ilya Altman, eds., *The Unknown Black Book: The Holocaust in the German-Occupied Soviet Territories* (Bloomington, IN: Indiana State University Press, 2008), 275–76.
7   Quoted in Friedländer, *Years of Extermination*, 407.
8   Quoted in Friedländer, *Years of Extermination*, 504.
9   As recounted by Irena Strzelecka, "Women," in Yisrael Gutman and Michael Berenbaum, eds., *Anatomy of the Auschwitz Death Camp* (Bloomington, IN: Indiana State University Press, 1994), 409–10.
10 Quoted in Benjamin Lieberman, *Terrible Fate: Ethnic Cleansing in the Making of Modern Europe* (Chicago, IL: Ivan R. Dee, 2006), 192.
11 Quoted in Lieberman, *Terrible Fate*, 210.
12 Quoted in Juliet Gardiner, *Wartime Britain 1939–1945* (London: Headline Book Publishing, 2004), 358.
13 Quoted in Peter Stansky, *The First Day of the Blitz: September 7, 1940* (New Haven, CT: Yale University Press, 2007), 139.
14 Quoted in Neil Gregor, "A *Schicksalgemeinschaft?* Allied Bombing, Civilian Morale, and Social Dissolution in Nuremberg, 1942–1945," *Historical Journal* 43:4 (2000): 1058–59.
15 Quoted in Nicholas Stargardt, *Witnesses of War: Children's Lives under the Nazis* (London: Jonathan Cape, 2005), 237–38.
16 See Stargardt, *Witnesses of War*, 249.
17 Quoted in Stargardt, *Witnesses of War*, 254.
18 Quoted in Gregor, "A *Schicksalgemeinschaft*," 1063.
19 Quoted in Morgan, *Fall of Mussolini*, 76.

20 As recounted in Haruko Taya Cook and Theodore Cook, eds., *Japan at War: An Oral History* (New York: The New Press, 1992), 348–49.

21 See Havens, *Valley of Darkness*, 185.

22 Quoted in Havens, *Valley of Darkness*, 190.

23 Quoted in Morgan, *Fall of Mussolini*, 138.

24 Quoted in William Hitchcock, *The Bitter Road to Freedom: A New History of the Liberation of Europe* (New York: Free Press, 2008), 22.

25 Richard Bessel, *Germany 1945: From War to Peace* (New York: Harper Collins, 2009), 138.

26 Juan Labrador, 18 February 1945, quoted in Richard Aldrich, ed., *The Faraway War: Personal Diaries of the Second World War in Asia and the Pacific* (London: Doubleday, 2005), 689–90.

27 See Andrew Rotter, *Hiroshima: The World's Bomb* (Oxford: Oxford University Press, 2008), 226–27.

28 Quoted in Aldrich, ed., *Faraway War*, 794–95.

4 | A World Unsettled

Though the Second World War formally ended with the surrender of Germany and Japan in 1945, its effects upon civilians reverberated for decades. For those living outside the battle zones, the end of hostilities brought an overwhelming sense of relief and great joy at the prospect of returning loved ones. But popular enthusiasm was tempered by the knowledge that many would not return, and veterans often found reintegration into civilian life very difficult. The wartime economy, and the challenges of wartime living, had brought a sense of purpose and even prosperity for some, but there was also anxiety about what lay ahead. Greater challenges awaited those living in defeated states and countries liberated from Axis rule. Here millions of people were dislocated and in desperate need of food and shelter. Though in retrospect the shift from penury to prosperity was comparatively swift in countries such as West Germany and Japan, the first postwar years in these countries—and for the peoples who had recently suffered under their rule—were harsh, with ordinary men, women, and children struggling to survive while living with the trauma of their wartime experiences.

In countries such as the United States, Britain, and Canada many hoped that the sacrifices made by ordinary citizens would lead to a more just political and social order. In the Soviet Union, the partial relaxation of political controls during the war nourished hopes that this trend would persist. In countries that had experienced Axis occupation survival was a major preoccupation, but the war also led to much soul-searching about how to reform society. Nationalist passions, heightened in response to the humiliation of foreign rule, remained potent in 1945 and long afterwards. This was perhaps even more the case in the European colonial empires than in Europe itself. In Africa calls for better conditions and greater autonomy grew louder; in the Middle East and Asia demands for independence reached a fever pitch.

Powerful and consequential as these demands for change were, many people wished for nothing more than to live a "normal" life. At the end of the war both governments and citizens in the United States and the British Commonwealth often made clear that they wanted a return to familiar patterns of social relations and domestic life. Comparable impulses were at work in the countries of Western Europe, where desires for a more egalitarian social order confronted demands for stability and drawing a curtain over the recent past so that people could move on. This desire for greater stability did much to modify, even check, passions for radical reform. Yet the changes wrought by the war could not be undone. The social structures of Eastern Europe had been shattered, facilitating the imposition of Communist rule. Comparable trends in China affected the outcome of the civil war that broke out there in 1946. European desires to restore imperial control ran headlong into desires for national independence, resulting in often protracted conflict.

Another factor of critical importance during this period was the break-up of the wartime alliance between the British Empire, the United States, and the Soviet Union. In 1945–46 the Americans and the British became convinced that the Soviets were set upon expansion in Europe, the Middle East, and Asia. For their part the Soviets, determined to construct a buffer zone in Eastern Europe and to prevent a revival of German power, believed that the capitalist West sought to encircle them. By 1947 the Cold War was underway. Its leading antagonists were the United States and the Soviet Union, but it had profound consequences for many nations. In the United States, Britain, and Western Europe the struggle against Communism brought renewed political mobilization. In the Soviet Union Stalin demanded more sacrifices from his people. Emerging Cold War tensions also shaped the consolidation of Communist power in Eastern Europe; the treatment of refugees; the reconstruction of Western European societies; the fate of divided nations such as Greece, Korea, and China; and struggles between European imperialists and anti-colonial nationalists.

The Victors: The British Empire, the United States, and the Soviet Union

The British people were elated by news of Germany's surrender. As one London housewife exclaimed on 7 May 1945, "I can't grasp the fact that it's all over. We've been bombed out twice, and we've got no roof over our heads, only a sheet of tarpaulin. My boy's home on leave after being away for nearly five years, but tomorrow I don't care what happens. I'm going to be really happy. I'm glad of the opportunity to relieve my pent-up feelings."[1] This combination of shock, relief at having endured a gruelling war effort, and raised expectations for the future made itself evident throughout the British Isles in myriad ways.

There was no hiding the fact that Britons had been stretched very thin and that the country was exhausted; the national debt was four times its prewar level, and the country was heavily reliant upon economic support from the United States. Despite these serious challenges, as well as wartime shortages and regulations, the elimination of unemployment and the availability of overtime work meant that working-class families were better off at war's end than at its outbreak. Rationing and measures such as the introduction of school meals and subsidized British Restaurants meant that nutritional levels across social classes also improved. A widespread desire to see that the state continued to apply itself to achieving better health, secure employment, and social reform helps to explain the triumph of the British Labour Party in the general election of July 1945, following the breakup of Churchill's wartime coalition government. A substantial lead in the popular vote—47.8 per cent for Labour versus 39.8 per cent for Churchill's Conservatives—translated into a landslide in terms of seats, empowering the new government to move ahead with ambitious legislation nationalizing key sectors of industry, building new public housing, and creating the National Health Service.

Historians have cautioned against overstating the radicalism of what happened in Britain in 1945, noting that many of those who voted Labour sought modest as opposed to revolutionary improvements in their daily lives. Britain continued to be a class society in crucial ways. The 1944 Education Bill, for instance, facilitated access to education by providing free transport and grants for poor children but also created three types of secondary school, with placement determined by an exam administered to 11-year-olds. The grammar schools, aimed at producing the majority of graduates intended for the universities, continued to be favoured over secondary schools oriented towards technical training. It has also been widely noted that despite the opportunities opened up for women by war-time employment, there was a strong drive towards reasserting familiar roles when the conflict ended. One manifestation of this was a predictable increase in marriage and birth rates, but official policy also went in this direction. State provisions for nurseries were quickly cut as the war wound down, making it more difficult for mothers of small children to engage in part-time work.

The desire to return to a comfortable "stability" in class and gender relations was clearly powerful, but the impact of the conflict could not easily be shaken off. Britain's economic difficulties meant that public housing construction did not proceed according to expectations and that rationing of some goods persisted into the 1950s. Some items that had not been affected during the conflict, such as potatoes, were placed on coupons following a very difficult winter in 1947. While austerity could lead to a sense of malaise, the war seems to have changed some attitudes, notably with respect to women. Despite the fact that, especially in traditionally "male" sectors like metals, chemicals, and engineering, the wartime employment of women was widely regarded as a stop-gap, employers did grow more amenable to the idea of hiring women part-time because of the lower costs. Most significantly, substantial numbers of women wished to continue in paid employment after the war. A 1943 Government Social Survey found that 39 per cent of married women wished to remain in paid work, full or part-time, after the war, compared to 36 per cent who did not; the percentage of married women with children wanting paid work was even higher, 49 per cent. In addition to the income, analysts found that many women appreciated the camaraderie of work and the escape it could offer from sometimes isolating domesticity. As Mona Marshall, a nursemaid who became a steelworker, put it: "It made me stand on my own two feet, gave me more self confidence."[2]

Canadians, too, emerged from the war with strong desires for stability, but they were more prepared to see government intervene to ensure the public good. Government officials had begun planning early for postwar demobilization, and the Veterans' Charter provided pensions, funded vocational training and university education, and furnished grants to promote farming and small business. This did not free Canadian families from the difficulties of adjusting to postwar life, sometimes without a father or husband, or with one traumatized by overseas experiences. The 47,783 "war brides," most of them British, who came to Canada found adjusting to a new country and to spouses whom they often did not really know very well difficult, but most stayed and built lasting marriages. The assistant national commissioner for the Canadian Red Cross observed, as early as January 1947, that "Our impression [is] that the percentage of shattered romances among these couples is negligible."[3] Within a country that had grown richer, rather than poorer, as a result of the conflict, many Canadian women shared with their British counterparts a stronger desire to remain in paid employment; thousands of former military women took advantage of veterans' retraining programs as well.

Comparable patterns emerged in Australia and New Zealand, which had both experienced economic growth and an unsettling of social relations. As we saw in Chapter 1, however, not everyone shared in the benefits of wartime social change to an equal extent. For example, while New Zealand's Prime Minister Peter Fraser stressed how the war had forged a new, more equitable relationship between the Maoris and New Zealanders of European extraction, this expressed more of an aspiration than a reality. Similar observations can be made regarding Canada's First Nations and Australia's Aborigines.

While the three dominions emerged from the war in generally stable condition, in Britain's vast colonial holdings the war highlighted the fragility of London's grip. Unlike Burma and Malaya, India had avoided invasion but certainly not turmoil. As we have seen, after failing to conciliate the Indian National Congress with promises of postwar independence, the British used force to suppress the "Quit India" movement in 1942, imprisoning Gandhi, Nehru, and tens of thousands of lesser known officials and supporters. This reduced the level of protest but did not eliminate the underlying tensions, and as the war came to a close parts of India were in chaos. In 1946 elements of the navy mutinied, as did hundreds of police, and over the course of that same year there were 1,629 industrial disputes involving some 2 million workers. Some of these protests were localized in nature and centred upon social issues, but the depth of hostility to British rule and the desire for Indian independence was unmistakeable. As the British governor of India's Central Provinces and Behar reported, "I am bound to say that I cannot recollect any period in which there has been such venomous and unbridled attacks against Government and Government officers."[4] Britain's decision to try former officers of the Japanese-sponsored Indian National Army, consisting largely of former POWs who decided to fight for the Great East Asia Co-Prosperity Sphere, further inflamed Indian nationalist opinion.

In addition to violence against the officials and symbols of the Raj, communal tensions between Hindus and Muslims were also mounting, a problem that British wartime political tactics had exacerbated. Given the strength of opposition from the Hindu-dominated Congress Party, the British had encouraged the growth of the venerable (established 1906) but hitherto relatively weak Muslim League, led by Muhammad Ali Jinnah. By 1940 the League championed the creation of a homeland for India's Muslims—Pakistan. For their part, the British indicated that they would not force a minority to become part of an Indian state. Beginning in December 1945 India-wide elections were held to provide a basis for discussing its future. With the Congress leading in non-Muslim districts and the Muslim League polling very well among its intended support base, the stage was set for acrimonious negotiations that culminated in the 1947 partition of India into two states, a process accompanied by violence that took hundreds of thousands of lives.

In the Middle East, too, British power was challenged by growing nationalism. In Egypt the ruling Wafd Party passed social legislation and allowed the formation of trade unions, but its legitimacy was tarnished by the fact that it had taken office in 1942 only after British tanks had surrounded the royal palace and compelled the king to name a favourable government. In the meantime, opposition forces, notably the Muslim Brotherhood, gained strength by championing Egyptian renewal according to the precepts of Islam and promoting social reform. As the war came to an end, elements of the Brotherhood engaged in attacks upon foreigners, as well as Egyptian officials whom they deemed guilty of promoting foreign interests; their victims included Prime Minister Mahmud Fahmi al-Nuqrashi, killed in 1948. Repression of the Brotherhood only led to further instability, which continued until King Farouk was toppled in a military coup in 1952. In Iraq the British had forcibly installed a government more sympathetic to their interests in 1941, but its key figures, Regent Abd al-Ilah and Nuri al-Sa'id, found their alignment with Britain to be a political liability after 1945; they were overthrown in a bloody coup in 1958.

Most tenuous of all, from the British perspective, was the situation in Palestine. London's 1939 decision to sharply curtail Jewish immigration had led Zionist leaders to conclude that Britain would no longer support the creation of a Jewish homeland; thus, it would have to be seized by force. In 1944 militant independent militias—the Irgun and Lehi (the Stern Gang)—had begun a terror campaign against the British; in 1945 the Haganah, the armed force of the more moderate Jewish Agency, joined in. Ongoing sabotage and spectacular attacks such as the Irgun-sponsored bombing of the King David Hotel in Jerusalem in 1946, led the overwhelmed British to refer the Palestinian "question" to the United Nations in 1947. They terminated the mandate in 1948. In May of that year the Zionist leadership proclaimed the independence of the new state of Israel and immediately found themselves at war with their Arab neighbours.

Nationalist sentiment was less intense in the British territories of sub-Saharan Africa, but here too the war had raised expectations for change. The intensified demands of the colonial state for African resources, especially when territories in Asia had been under Japanese control, had encouraged economic expansion, rapid urban growth, and inflation, causing dislocation and sometimes disaffection. At the same time, local demands for greater autonomy intensified. In 1943, for example, a group of West African journalists delivered a memorandum to the Colonial Office in London that forecast their states becoming full members of the Commonwealth within 15 years. The return home of hundreds of thousands of African soldiers also had a considerable impact. Though not all had been politicized by their wartime service, some were, and dissatisfaction with the conditions of their demobilization and with ongoing colonial rule caused political unrest. A key example of this was the case of veterans who protested in Accra (Gold Coast/Ghana) in 1948 and who were fired upon by police. The subsequent rioting and violence left nearly 30 dead and hundreds injured. The incident pushed the British to introduce political reforms, though at the time they did not envisage the Gold Coast achieving independence as soon as it did, in 1957.

Within the self-governing dominion of South Africa, by contrast, wartime social change provoked a sharp racialist backlash. A wartime economic boom and the need for African labour brought hundreds of thousands of new urban settlers to shantytowns on the outskirts of cities such as Johannesburg. These migrants began to mobilize in large numbers; by 1945 the Council of Non-European Trade Unions claimed a membership of 158,000. Strikes and protests aimed at securing improvements to a miserable standard of living frightened many South African whites, who in 1948 elected the hard-line National Party, which moved to intensify racial segregation through the implementation of the apartheid system.

The peoples of the British Empire thus emerged from the war exhausted, hopeful, and impatient in varying degrees. The population of the United States emerged buoyed by a major national achievement, but it was also anxious about the future. Having entered the war still suffering from worrisome unemployment and economic troubles, at the time of the German and Japanese surrenders the United States was the richest country in the world. Wartime mobilization eliminated unemployment and led to massive changes in the workforce, creating opportunities for women and ethnic minorities. One African-American resident of Richmond, California—a community that experienced rapid growth and migration from the Southern States—recalled how, "It was exciting, fun to be with different types of people. I really felt free."[5] One of the millions of American women who found wartime work rewarding countered demands for a restoration of "traditional values" by commenting that, "War jobs have uncovered unsuspected abilities in the American woman. Why lose all these abilities because of a belief that 'a woman's place is in the home'? For some it is, for others not."[6]

Many Americans did worry, however, about the state of the economy after the war. Though the boom increased national wealth, it also promoted economic concentration. Larger companies tended to get more government contracts while thousands of smaller firms went under; the number of farms in the United States decreased by 17 per cent, the result of declining numbers of smaller family operations. And although the years ahead would in fact be characterized by prosperity for many, in 1945–46 there were widespread fears that the end of wartime mobilization would be followed by an economic downturn. A December 1944 poll, inquiring whether US citizens believed that everyone who wanted a job would be able to get one, elicited a 68 per cent negative response. Large numbers of Americans were also unnerved by the social disruptions of the war years. Many commentators felt that youth were running wild, the result of a lack of parental guidance and their increased spending power, which was fed by the growth in jobs for the young. There was perhaps even greater concern about the condition of marriage. Given the often brief courtships that preceded some trips down the wedding aisle, as well as lengthy separations and the temptations of infidelity both for those serving overseas but also spouses and sweethearts at home, it is not surprising that both marriage and divorce rates skyrocketed.

Thus, for countless families in the United States the shift from war to peace was challenging. The GI Bill, passed into law in June 1944, certainly eased the transition, by allowing some 8 million veterans to receive further education or job training after the war. But even if the resumption of civilian life was buffered by relative economic security—and that was not always the case—money was of little help in addressing other challenges. Many demobilized soldiers felt alienated from their fellow citizens. The writer William Manchester, who had served in the Marines, observed that his comrades felt that what they had accomplished was "of immense historical import, and that those of us who survived it would be forever cherished in the hearts of Americans. It was rather diminishing to return in 1945 and discover that your own parents couldn't even pronounce the names of the islands you had conquered."[7] Beyond desires for recognition and empathy were worries about rekindling the most intimate of relationships. Would wives and sweethearts still embrace them? Would their children be afraid of them, even remember them? Many servicemen struggled to adjust to the routines of work and family life; for the disfigured or disabled veteran doing so was even more difficult. Betty Bayse Hutchinson, who served as a nurse, recalled a man who had lost his nose, then learned that his wife was going to divorce him: "The doctor wanted her to understand it'll take time, he'll get his face back. But they broke up. She couldn't stand it. That was pretty common."[8]

As the war ended there was a strong push towards reasserting the centrality of domestic life in the United States. Commercial advertising urged wives to remain desirable for returning husbands. A Palmolive commercial featuring a young woman and a soldier asked, "When he comes home to you, will he find you as lovely as his heart has dreamed you'd be?" Using Palmolive would help women to "guard [their] loveliness."[9] However appealing a wife remained, many returning servicemen wanted them at home, even if they had previously worked; many veterans feared that women might retain jobs at their expense. Wartime advertising and government propaganda also encouraged Americans to view wartime employment for women as temporary. As production lines began the transition from war to peace, disproportionately large numbers of female workers found themselves out of a job. For some this was not something to be regretted—they wished to focus on their families. Yet there is evidence that a significant number of women in war work valued the experience—a 1944 survey conducted by the War Manpower Commission found that more than half of all married women workers indicated that they would like to keep their jobs so long as it was not at the expense of a returning veteran. Such opinions were voiced, however, within an increasingly conservative climate. Though the 1923 Equal Rights Amendment, which made all sexual discrimination constitutionally illegal, came before Congress in 1946, it did not receive enough support from the Senate to move on to the states for ratification. A 1946 poll found that seven-eighths of respondents felt that homemaking was a "full-time job." Clearly there was a renewed emphasis upon domesticity in the early postwar era, though it would be contested by the daughters of the World War Two generation as they came of age in the 1960s and 1970s.

This conservative turn in gender relations was part of a broader shift. Discredited by the Great Depression, the reputation of big business in the United States was rehabilitated by its wartime performance, and while unions remained active, class-based politics was frequently chastised. By 1947 emerging Cold War tensions led to renewed calls for unity and discipline when it came to confronting Communism; suspicion of leftists in the United States intensified, culminating in the McCarthyism of the early 1950s. And while wartime propaganda had stressed national unity and commitment to tolerance, ethnic tensions persisted. Standards of living for African-American veterans remained below those of their white counterparts, while in the South racial segregation endured for two more decades. Yet the desire for reform was far from extinguished. For instance, the National Association for the Advancement of Colored People (NAACP) expanded rapidly during the war. Pressure from African-American activists such as A. Philip Randolph, founder of the International Brotherhood of Sleeping Car Porters, helped to convince President Harry Truman to order the desegregation of the US military in 1948. This was an important step in the direction of greater civil rights.

While the United States experienced a contested revival of conservative values at the end of the war, the citizens of the Soviet Union quickly discovered that Stalin's regime was determined to reassert a tight grip over them. The Soviet Union demobilized most of its troops very quickly—by 1948 8.5 million men and women had left military life, out of a total of 11.4 million people under arms in 1945. Many were terribly anxious to see their loved ones again, but other marriages were haunted by deception. This was the case with one Moscow couple, Valentina and Valya, who were reunited in 1946 after Valya finished his term with occupation forces in Germany. The couple remained together until Valya's death in 2001, but during his service in Germany he had had an affair, and a child, with a German woman, whom he abandoned when his service ended. Reviewing her correspondence with the historian Catherine Merridale decades later, Valentina remarked, "I don't mind the old letters. But they were such lies. All that stuff about love and homesickness. All the time he was with her, the German woman."[10] Since married couples had preferential access to their own apartments in the postwar Soviet Union, even though Valentina had found out about the affair early on, she stayed with Valya for decades.

Such relationships were further strained by difficult living conditions. Much of the western Soviet Union was devastated. In addition to the loss of perhaps 25 million of its citizens, it had sustained the destruction of 70,000 villages and 1,700 towns; major cities such as Stalingrad and Leningrad had been laid waste. Millions of Soviet POWs had perished in German captivity, though perhaps 1 million did return home after the fighting. In addition, some 5.5 million Soviet citizens, many brought to the Reich as slave labourers, were repatriated between 1945 and 1953. They came home to a hungry nation. After a severe drought and harvest failure in 1946, the prices of most goods were tripled in September 1946, and rationing of food and manufactured items lasted until 1947. The situation did not really improve until the end of the decade, after price cuts were introduced. Under these conditions crime and social unrest became serious problems, belying an official image of continuing order. A letter by a group of workers in the city of Saratov to the newspaper *Pravda* complained that "since the beginning of fall [1945] Saratov has been terrorized by thieves and murderers. To be forced to undress on the street, to have watches snatched from the wrist has become an everyday occurrence.... The life of the city simply ceases as darkness approaches."[11]

Amid the harsh conditions, Soviet citizens took pride in the leading role their country had played in the defeat of Nazi Germany, though their pride sometimes verged upon arrogance. The veteran Fedor Abramov put it in the following terms: "Drunk with the conceit of victory, we decided that our system was ideal ... and we not only neglected to improve it, we grew ever more dogmatic about it."[12] Strident patriotism was not the only theme of postwar rhetoric, however. Many Soviet citizens, especially younger ones, hoped the postwar era would bring a relaxation of rigid controls. The regime had adopted a more pragmatic stance during the war with Germany, showing, for example, more tolerance for religious practice. The popular mood, to the extent that it can be discerned, appears to have favoured further liberalization. One Soviet writer hopefully (and naïvely) remarked in 1944 that, "When the war is over, life in Russia will become very pleasant. There will be much coming and going, with a lot of contact with the West. Everybody will be allowed to read anything he likes. There will be exchanges of students, and foreign travel will be made easy."[13] Such desires for a better future also led to complaints about the Soviet system. These rarely involved criticisms of Stalin himself; fear and the propaganda machine seem to have largely shielded the dictator from popular reproach. But criticism of party officials was audible; official reports recorded comments such as, "What good can we expect when the government and the party are robbing each other? That is why our life is so difficult."[14]

Life remained very difficult for years. As historian Sheila Fitzpatrick observes, though much of the Red Army was demobilized after the war, Soviet society was not.[15] In addition to rationing, stringent controls were maintained upon an exhausted labour force. Millions were drafted to work on reconstruction projects or sent to tackle difficult assignments such as working in the Siberian coal mines. Labour reserve schools provided an additional source of workers, with 3.6 million students passing through them between 1946 and 1950. The regime also continued to employ millions of convicts, now joined by Axis prisoners of war. As for the millions of people repatriated to the Soviet Union in the wake of the war, a substantial proportion of them did not want to go back. Some had willingly collaborated with the Third Reich, to the point of serving it in uniform, but others rightly feared that having been drafted to work in Germany marked them as potentially disloyal. The Western Allies frequently honoured Soviet demands to hand these people over, despite disturbing results. About one-fifth of the 2.2 million who did return wound up in prison and in some cases were executed.

The Soviets also moved ruthlessly to assert control over the new territories they had annexed during the war, notably the Baltic States and lands taken from Poland and Romania. Hundreds of thousands of Soviet citizens—mainly Russians, many of them recently demobilized soldiers—were resettled in these areas to ensure a reliable presence. Measures such as the collectivization of agriculture soon followed. Local populations sometimes responded with fierce resistance. Baltic and Ukrainian nationalists waged guerrilla warfare on Soviet forces and pro-Soviet elements, with fighting lasting into the late 1940s. The Soviet wartime policy of fostering Russian national sentiment had encouraged a more rigid sense of ethnic identity, and these conflicts further promoted it. Though the regime's ideology strictly condemned biological racism, official discourse could be blatantly xenophobic. In particular, anti-Jewish sentiment was on the rise after the war ended, nurtured by Stalin's own increasing paranoia about a plot against his life by "Jewish doctors." Overall, the public mood in the Soviet Union remained very uneasy, and the onset of the Cold War with the West only heightened the climate of repression. As long as Stalin lived, he demanded strict regimentation. Even after his death in 1953, controls were only relaxed to an extent.

The Aftermath of Hitler's New Order

In 1945 Europe was a continent emerging from unprecedented destruction. Though some urban centres such as Paris, Rome, and Prague had escaped large-scale damage, tens of millions of people—an estimated 20 million in the German lands alone—were left homeless by bomb and battle damage. Key transportation networks were in ruins. In France only 2,800 out of a prewar total of 12,000 locomotives remained serviceable in the spring of 1945, while two-thirds of the country's merchant fleet had been sunk. Food shortages were another serious problem, given the widescale destruction of crops and the death of millions of livestock. Yugoslavia, for instance, lost 60 per cent of its horses and over half of its cattle, sheep, goats, and poultry. Everywhere the loss of life and property was enormous, but the toll of German occupation had been particularly heavy in the East. Whereas countries like France, Holland, and Belgium lost between 10 and 20 per cent of their national incomes, in Poland and Yugoslavia the proportion was closer to 50 per cent. Grim though it is to make comparisons, the same can be said in terms of loss of life—over 200,000 civilian deaths occurred in Holland and 350,000 in France, while in Poland and Yugoslavia the totals were near 5 million and 1.4 million deaths, respectively.

Europe was also experiencing a massive refugee crisis. At the end of the war there were millions of "displaced persons" (DPs)—those who had been forcibly or accidentally separated from their families—roaming the continent, primarily in the German lands. Among them were former concentration camp prisoners, foreign workers—often slave labourers—and survivors of the Holocaust. Working in conjunction with various international aid organizations, the new United Nations Relief and Rehabilitation Administration (UNRRA) tried to care for the DPs, running hundreds of camps for them. Many DPs—especially those from Western Europe—wished to return home as soon as possible and were repatriated in relatively short order. But millions of Soviet citizens and other East Europeans did not want to go home, for fear of persecution by the Communist authorities. Though initially many were forced to return, as Cold War tensions mounted, some 1.5 million East Europeans avoided forced repatriation. Many of them eventually moved to Western European countries, the United States, Canada, and Australia.

Given what they had endured under the Nazis, and the persecution they faced even in the early postwar years, the experience of Jewish DPs requires separate explanation. Traumatized by their experiences, they sometimes endured confinement in camps alongside people who had persecuted them. Given what had happened, many did not wish to return home; indeed, the Jewish population of the DP camps actually expanded after the war, as some 220,000 East European Jews fled west. A key reason for this was the persistence of anti-Semitic violence, nourished by religious prejudices but also political and racist convictions and, in some cases, the fear that surviving Jews might seek to reclaim property taken by their neighbours. Pogroms occurred in a number of states after the war, the most infamous of which occurred in Kielce, Poland in July 1946, where 42 people were killed following accusations that Jews had abducted a Christian child to carry out "ritual murder." It took years, but ultimately Jews were able to leave the DP camps. A total of 330,000 people immigrated to Israel between 1948 and 1951, while another 165,000 moved to Britain, France, Australia, and the Americas.

Those who left Europe during these years departed a continent increasingly divided by tensions between the Western allies and the Soviet Union; the division was particularly stark in occupied Germany. By prior agreement during the war, the defeated Reich was divided into four occupation zones, controlled by the United States, Britain, France, and the Soviet Union. In theory the partition was to be temporary, but before long the diverging approaches of the British and the Americans on one hand and the Soviets on the other made this seem increasingly unlikely. Facing severe economic problems, and fearing that a desperate population would turn to Communism, the British and Americans soon decided to revive capitalist economic activity and eventually self-government. The Soviets, by contrast, sought to establish a state-run economy in their zone; they also removed vast quantities of goods and infrastructure as reparations and carried out measures such as the expropriation of landed estates.

German politicians who had survived the war years in silence, prison, hiding, or exile now found themselves working with either the Soviets or the Western Allies, according to their situation and ideological goals. Communists such as Walter Ulbricht worked with the Soviets to build what would soon be a one-party state. In the western zones, Social Democrats such as Kurt Schumacher stressed the need for social reform within the context of renewed democratic freedoms while the Christian Democrats, led by Konrad Adenauer, wanted democracy too, but also a more religiously inspired society, which would tolerate class divisions while rejecting class warfare. What emerged from these competing visions were two very different German states. The western zones were gradually merged into what became the Federal Republic of Germany (FRG), which was formally established in May 1949. That October, the former Soviet zone became the German Democratic Republic (GDR).

The actions of the occupying powers were crucial in shaping institutions and outcomes, but the decisions of ordinary Germans—to adapt, to move on, and often to forget what their country had done—also weighed in the balance. The legacy of Nazism was grim; Germany had lost nearly 5 million men of military age, which meant that the burden of rebuilding fell upon a disproportionately female society in which single parents were numerous. Moreover, the western zones of occupied Germany soon had to accommodate some 12 million German refugees from the east, which included communities that had fled the Red Army, as well as ethnic Germans expelled from countries like Poland and Czechoslovakia.

In what became the FRG US, British, and French occupation forces found the population focused on day-to-day survival and strongly inclined to regard themselves as victims, with any recognition of what their nation had done diminished by recent memories of bombing, invasion, and expulsion. At first the Allies devoted much energy to de-Nazification, an initiative greeted with considerable hostility by many Germans. But the need for trained personnel and to rebuild soon blunted this process, meaning that many former servants of the Third Reich went on to successful careers in the FRG. With fears of social and political radicalism and the desire—especially on the part of financially stretched Britain—to make the German economy self-sustaining, the Allies increasingly encouraged capitalist economic reconstruction, for despite wartime destruction there was potential for recovery. Some firms, such as Volkswagen, survived with most of their machinery intact. In June 1945 only 10 per cent of German railways were operational; a year later 93 per cent of all German railway tracks had been reopened. Elections, first permitted by the Allies at the local and regional levels, then finally at the national level, resulted in a victory for Adenauer's Christian Democrats in 1949. Notwithstanding the shattering of many "traditional" families, the Christian Democrats stressed the need for family order and economic recovery, calling upon voters to "help to construct a new and more beautiful Germany upon the unshakeable foundations of Christianity and of Western culture."[16] Though popular support for the left-leaning SPD served as a reminder that alternative visions were on offer, the appeal of the Christian Democrats attests to the hunger for stability.

In the GDR, by contrast, the new Communist authorities, who had to contend with a populace simmering with hostility towards the Red Army, focused more on carrying out social and economic reforms they believed would uproot the structures that had given rise to Nazism. East Germans were also expected to pour their energies into rebuilding but within a context where land had been redistributed and factories nationalized. However, in spite of the fact that official ideology stressed the "anti-fascist" foundations of the GDR, the East German Communists also had to accommodate hundreds of thousands of citizens tainted by association with Nazism. There was a significant purge of officials in the early postwar years—over 500,000 individuals by 1948—but the GDR also had to make use of large numbers of ex-Nazis in order to run the machinery of state. In the 1960s more than 10 per cent of the deputies in the East German parliament had previously been Nazi Party members. East Germany did emerge from the war a profoundly different society, but the new system imposed by the Communists could not help but draw upon its predecessor in some ways.

By the 1950s the countries of Western Europe that had experienced Nazi occupation had for the most part also embraced political and economic systems oriented towards stability and economic reconstruction, but only a few years before such an outcome was not obvious. Though the degree of damage and volatility was not as extensive in, say, Denmark as in Holland, France, or Italy, food shortages, inflation, unemployment, and unrest were pervasive at the war's end. The desire for revenge upon collaborators had resulted in a good deal of rough justice in 1944–45 before restored state authorities could truly reassert control. In France about 10,000 former collaborators were killed as a result of popular violence and makeshift tribunals; in Italy the figure was probably closer to 15,000. Another phenomenon, which has drawn growing attention from historians in recent years, was the punishment of women suspected of engaging in sexual relations with the enemy. Many of them experienced public humiliation—frequently in the form of head-shaving or some form of marking—as well as physical abuse. The thousands of children born of unions between German soldiers and local women often faced an uncertain future. Even those in relatively stable family settings often had to contend with the confusion of unspoken family secrets.

The strong desire for change, to break utterly with the discredited systems of the past, had major political implications. The Neapolitan paper *La Voce* captured this yearning when it declared on 8 May 1945, "We shall not forget! We shall destroy fascism forever! Only thus will the world be reborn from the ruins and go forward towards a future of peace, progress, justice and freedom."[17] Not surprisingly, in the early postwar years the popular mood in Western Europe swung to the left. Socialists were now well-positioned to influence policy, but truly striking was the fact that Communist parties—their image burnished by their emphasis upon antifascism and resistance activities—did better electorally than ever before. They scored nearly 20 per cent of the vote in Italian elections held in 1946;

the French Communists achieved their all-time peak that same year, 28.6 per cent of the vote. The political landscape was also transformed by the fact that in France, Italy, and Belgium women were voting at the national level for the first time. And while these new voters displayed a range of political opinions, it is also noteworthy how at the time most political parties also responded to popular expectations for a better life by embracing the cause of social reform. Though significant differences between left and right remained, in the main, demands for an end to unemployment through state planning, and the expansion of social security, were at the heart of a broad political consensus.

This led to major economic and social reforms in many countries. The new British Labour government nationalized a number of key industries on the grounds that they should serve the public as a whole and that the state could run them more effectively to that end. One-fifth of France's industrial capacity was state-owned by 1946. The introduction or enhancement of government-run social insurance plans was a prominent feature of early postwar reform as well. And while US aid, particularly after the approval of the Marshall Plan launched in 1947, was geared towards boosting productivity, creating wealth, and thereby blunting the appeal of Communism, many US officials conceded the importance of Europeans having a social safety net. A new political consensus, characterized by greater state intervention and management to ensure high employment and better social services, took shape.

The desire to break with a discredited old order sometimes led to major institutional changes as well, such as the replacement of Belgium's king, compromised by his behaviour during the occupation, and the abolition of the Italian monarchy, tainted by association with Mussolini, in a referendum. However, the fact that both measures were controversial serves as a reminder that the shift to the left, though appreciable, was not universal. Moreover, it must also be remembered that most Western and Mediterranean European nations had been liberated by the Western Allies, who desired reconstruction but would not countenance revolution. How far they would go to curb radicalism quickly became evident in Greece, where the growing power and political militancy of the left-wing resistance group EAM and its military wing ELAS alarmed elements of Greek society, as well as officials in London. In December 1944 fighting between ELAS and anti-Communists broke out in Athens, with the British intervening on the side of the latter. When, in 1947, financial troubles made it impossible for the British to sustain their role, the United States stepped in with financial assistance and advisers. Civil war would continue until 1949, when the left was defeated; repression of its supporters continued for years afterwards.

Admittedly, the Greek case was an extreme one. In other countries some resisters may have been radicalized by their wartime experiences, but they were not in a position to reach for power. Stalin left the Greek Communists to their fate, and for nearly two years after the end of the war, he urged their counterparts in France and Italy to avoid radicalism and to cooperate with other political formations in coalition governments devoted to reconstruction, which they did. But in 1947, amid rising Cold War tensions and disputes over priorities within these reformist coalitions, the French and Italian Communists were forced into opposition. A growing sense of disillusionment accompanied the fragmentation of these coalitions; many former resisters felt that the chance to achieve profound change had been squandered. Even more conservative observers, such as the French Catholic writer François Mauriac, were promoting a nostalgic view of the German Occupation as early as 1946: "Do you not sometimes think ... of those sombre days with a secret nostalgia? ... Certainly those days of horror were not good days. But they were days of friendship and confidence...."[18]

As West European politics gradually shifted to the right, the drive to punish collaborators also lost momentum. Practical considerations were at work here; in Italy, where Mussolini's Fascists had ruled for over 20 years, and where civil servants had been required to join, it was soon concluded that trying to punish everyone associated with the regime would at best produce paralysis and at worst civil war. In France roughly 38,000 people were imprisoned at the end of the war for treason and related offences; by 1951 all but 1,500 of them were free. Here again, ensuring continuity in the administration and the desire to avoid excessive political polarization were key priorities.

While demands for democratization and social reform were powerful in Western Europe, so were desires for national renewal, which for some countries entailed an effort to revive their imperial glory. The French carried out some social and political reforms in their colonies, stressing the need to address the well-being of local populations and their greater participation in government, but refused to countenance true independence. Algerian nationalist demonstrations carried out on VE-Day in 1945 and that turned violent were suppressed with great brutality at the cost of thousands of lives. By the end of the following year, France was engaged in a prolonged but ultimately fruitless quest to reassert control over Vietnam. Eight years later, in 1954, an Algerian nationalist insurrection sparked another prolonged, immensely destructive colonial war, terminated only in 1962 when Algeria achieved full independence. In both Vietnam and Algeria the war had done much to strengthen desires for independence, but the majority of France's political class had also concluded that empire was required for national regeneration in the postwar era, setting the stage for confrontation. Similarly, the Dutch initially tried to regain control over their prized possessions in Indonesia, only to confront powerful nationalist opposition, which ultimately prevailed.

Despite such ongoing conflicts, by the early 1950s West European economies and societies entered a new phase in which the impact of wartime devastation became less evident. Growth started to take hold, democratic if flawed political systems began to consolidate, and birth rates rose. A cigarette advertisement in the West German weekly *Stern* dated 2 May 1954 offered a revealing commentary, even if its message seemed at odds with its goal of boosting sales:

> Behind us lie years that seem like a bad dream today.... We were in such dire straits that we did not hold life in high esteem anymore—life almost had lost its meaning!... For us, even an everyday requirement such as eating got a completely excessive value: everyone was obsessed with the idea of getting something to eat. Likewise we lusted after alcohol and nicotine.... [But] life is worth living again, and we again regard health as the supreme good. We have returned to those limits of pleasure that Goethe called the hallmark of the master. We no longer live without thinking of tomorrow.[19]

Though its announcement of prosperity would no doubt have seemed premature to many European families, in drawing attention to the psychological aftermath of total war while obscuring the details of what had happened, and promoting a return to self-discipline and long-term thinking, this advertisement in *Stern* arguably reflected the material and emotional distance travelled by many West Europeans within a decade.

Eastern Europe, as we have seen, suffered even greater devastation than the West. The loss of life was greatest in Poland and Yugoslavia, both of which had experienced severe occupations and internal ethnic strife. But countries that had initially opted to side with Germany in the war, such as Hungary and Romania, also experienced major wartime losses of 665,000 and 436,000 people respectively, which included civilians killed by bombing and in the final stages of fighting. Some elements of the population had suffered proportionately more than others; this was particularly the case for the region's large Jewish minorities, decimated by the Holocaust. Jews had played a crucial role in the economies and professions of many countries; they had provided Poland with half of its doctors and one-third of its lawyers and accounted for nearly 50 per cent of Romania's commercial classes. In many ways, the Jewish communities had been the backbone of the East European middle classes; their destruction was therefore profoundly destabilizing, as was the fact that the Nazi occupiers had targeted members of the professions and intelligentsia. The loss of such individuals rendered these societies more pliable to radical social change and necessarily created new opportunities for East Europeans from other backgrounds to rise through the ranks.

The end of hostilities did not bring an end to nationalist passions or popular violence. As we have already seen, anti-Semitism remained a potent force in the region. So was the desire for revenge upon Germany, as expressed by the expulsion of millions of ethnic Germans from Czechoslovakia, Poland, and elsewhere. These actions were frequently brutal; local Germans, often regardless of their past activities, received little notice that they had to leave and were allowed to take but a few possessions with them. Thefts, violence, and sexual assaults were frequent, especially in the earlier phases of the expulsions. In the last days of the war Czech partisans had seized control of a German radio station in Prague, which they promptly used to broadcast the message: "kill Germans wherever you meet them!"[20] By 1946 the process had become more "orderly," but was still often traumatic for those involved.

Alongside the cause of national revenge, cries for political and social change were also strong in most Eastern European countries. The right-wing governments that had led countries such as Hungary, Romania, and Bulgaria into disaster were discredited and toppled. The evisceration of the Polish Home Army in the Warsaw uprising weakened the counter-state built up by the resistance, while the failure of France and Britain to come to Czechoslovakia's aid before the war and the humiliations of occupation unsettled its previous pro-Western orientation. As various political systems were swept away or at least undermined, long-standing and more recent demands for social reform came to the surface. Since the end of the First World War there had been calls for extensive land reform to benefit the still largely peasant societies of the region, calls that had been only partially addressed by interwar governments and that remained potent in 1945. Furthermore, the sheer scale of wartime destruction compelled an extensive government role in guiding reconstruction. The nationalization of industry was one strategy for achieving this. Governments also often took control of assets from minorities that had been either murdered, notably Jews, or expelled, in the case of the Germans. Public support for nationalization of various industries was strong in many East European states, and such measures, along with land reform, were adopted even before the local Communist parties consolidated their dictatorships.

Thus, as in the West, there was an appreciable swing to the left by public opinion in much of Eastern Europe after the war, one that benefited reformist, Socialist, and even Communist movements. But between 1945 and 1948 those demands for change were monopolized and regimented by the Communists, who had significant, authentic popular support in some states. In Yugoslavia this was the result of Tito's resistance activities; at war's end he commanded 800,000 partisans and the Communist Youth League already had 150,000 members, a figure that skyrocketed in the following months. In Czechoslovakia the Communist Party had over 1 million supporters by the spring of 1946 and had won nearly 40 per cent of the popular vote in democratic national elections. Even in Hungary and Poland, where anti-Communist sentiment had been powerful since the interwar era, Communist party membership was approaching the half-million mark by 1946. But in neither country—nor in Bulgaria or Romania—was such support sufficient to ensure Communist governments would take shape of their own accord. Stalin was determined that Eastern Europe should serve as a buffer for the Soviet Union, especially if German power revived, as he feared it would. As relations with the Western democracies deteriorated, the coalition governments of Eastern Europe were replaced by Communist dictatorships, with Soviet officials and security forces often providing significant help to local Communists.

The timing and circumstances of the takeovers varied. Soviet power was of limited impact in Yugoslavia, where Tito quickly consolidated a one-party regime, repressing political alternatives and purging both former collaborators and potential rivals. In Poland, by contrast, the Soviet presence was critical. Here a coalition government gave way to a firmly Communist-dominated regime by 1947; this was achieved through the systematic use of force against thousands of anti-Communist insurgents, as well as repression and intimidation against non-Communist parties. Such tactics were also readily evident in Romania, whose Communists had been a tiny movement between the wars but, amid drastically changed circumstances and with Soviet support, achieved a commanding position in elections held in November 1946. This proved to be the key turning point, though Romania's king did not abdicate until the end of 1947. By that time non-Communist movements in Bulgaria and Hungary had also been decisively undermined. In winter 1948 Czechoslovakia, too, became a satellite of the Soviet Union. Though Communist support there remained substantial, by 1947 it was weakening, partially because Stalin vetoed Czechoslovakia's prospects for receiving Marshall Plan aid. In a context of rapidly deteriorating East-West relations and facing the prospect of losing votes in upcoming national elections, the Communists mobilized popular militias and trade union supporters. Rather than see his country torn apart by civil strife, President Edvard Beneš endorsed the formation of a new Communist-dominated administration, which quickly and forcefully consolidated its position.

For the next four decades, until the Revolutions of 1989, the countries of Eastern Europe would be governed by essentially one-party regimes, which exercised autocratic political control, oversaw command economies, and depended upon Soviet power. In most of the takeovers of the latter 1940s support from the Soviet Union was a decisive factor. Yet wartime upheavals had also led to political radicalization, which strengthened the electoral position and popular support of the Communists in some countries. More generally, the social legacy of the war also facilitated the new regimes' consolidation of power. The shattering of family and community bonds, as well as the displacement of populations, made large numbers of people more receptive to Communist Party demands to build a new and stable social order. The contrasting experience of workers in two Polish cities illustrates this point. In Łódź, within the boundaries of prewar Poland, local workers could draw upon a well-established tradition of labour activism, and they frequently contested Communist regimentation. By contrast, in Wrocław—until recently German Breslau—a largely new, resettled population of Poles from different parts of the country lacked communal traditions to draw upon, making it easier for the Communists to assert control over them.

The Former Japanese Empire

Though not invaded and conquered as Germany had been, Japan was devastated by heavy bombing, as well as the atomic strikes on Hiroshima and Nagasaki. The country's surrender left some 6.5 million Japanese "stranded" outside the home islands, in Manchuria, Korea, and elsewhere. Within a year most had "come home" to a country they had often never seen, though in the fall of 1946 there were still 2 million who had not returned. Some never would; there had been some 4,000 suicides among the Japanese settlers in

Manchuria alone following the Soviet invasion of 1945, and others were killed by vengeful local populations. In Japan itself people faced constant shortages and a pervasive condition of *kyodatsu*—"war exhaustion" or "despair." Vast numbers of Japanese veterans—an estimated 4.5 million—were listed as wounded or ill in 1945, a situation that made reintegration into family and civilian life all the more difficult. The extent to which everyday life was now characterized by the struggle to survive, and was being redefined by the presence of US occupation forces led by General Douglas MacArthur, was reflected in children's games; three of the most popular were simulating the black market, pretending to be GIs and prostitutes, and re-enacting left-wing and labour demonstrations.

The latter activity denotes that although life was very difficult and many Japanese had been traumatized by the shock of defeat, others saw the opportunities to effect radical reform. The writer Sakaguchi Ango argued in his 1946 essay "On Decadence" that, with the brutal fantasies of the wartime empire now destroyed, a humbled Japan offered far greater authenticity than its predecessor and the potential to realize a genuine humanity.[21] Sakaguchi was one of a growing number of voices stressing the need to rebuild the country along wholly different lines. Compared to the war years many Japanese believed that they now had greater personal freedom. Some of this took on a libertine quality—strip bars and nude shows featuring women posing as famous works of Western art inside large mock picture frames became popular—but social and political movements also gained momentum. Japan's labour unions had some 380,000 members at the end of 1945; by 1948 this had increased to an estimated 6.7 million. Support for the country's Socialist and Communist parties also grew appreciably. As the historian John Dower argues, popular enthusiasm for a radical remaking of Japan in a framework of "peace and democracy"—involving a complete break from the country's militarist past—was burgeoning.[22]

It was only allowed to go so far, however. The US occupation authorities sought both to democratize and demilitarize the country and to restore it as an economic power. Compared to the situation in Germany they had greater scope for action, as the other Allies played only a marginal role in the occupation of Japan. MacArthur's officials enacted some significant changes, including land reform, political rights for women, and the renunciation of war, a principle incorporated into Japan's 1947 constitution. But US authorities were also concerned with preserving social stability and discouraging labour unrest and political radicalism, especially as the Cold War loomed. Often unable to speak Japanese, they relied on local elites, many of whom were determined to retain a more hierarchical social structure. One important symbol of continuity with the old order lay in the constitution; while it vested sovereignty in the Japanese people, it retained the emperor as head of state. Toleration for strikes and protests also proved to be limited. MacArthur criticized mass demonstrations against the shortcomings of the food distribution system in May 1946 as the work of subversives, and by 1948 the occupiers were promoting anti-Communist sentiment within the labour movement. Thus, US officials, working with Japanese allies, ultimately established a conservative political system buttressed by impressive economic growth, though both only began to take root in the 1950s.

The Western powers proved less able to control the situation in Southeast Asia. In Vietnam and Indonesia the Japanese had fatally undermined French and Dutch imperial control. The Vietminh had seized power and declared independence; though working with rather than against the Japanese, Sukarno had done the same. By 1945 inflation, food shortages, and dislocation were rampant in both territories, and nationalist passions were palpable. Resident Europeans, already taken aback by the Japanese presence, often found that they could not reclaim their old lives. One contemporary, remarking on attempts by recently interned Dutch civilians to resume their old routines, discerned continuities with the past, but also real change:

> Some of [the Dutch civilians] succeeded in re-opening their houses and employing their former servants, and shopkeepers were polite and helpful. Sometimes all was not quite so friendly, a brusque refusal would indicate a more independent frame of mind, a Dutch man with a punctured bicycle tire would be told to mend it himself, a former faithful house boy would scorn domestic service.[23]

Both the Dutch and the French governments sought to reassert their colonial positions, and both had international support in this regard. Nationalist Chinese forces loyal to Jiang Jieshi's regime took the Japanese surrender in northern Vietnam, while British troops temporarily occupied the south. The Chinese were unsympathetic to the French, but the British were far more accommodating, and by the time they withdrew in 1946 the French had a strong presence in the south. Europeans displayed an air of confidence there, and suspected Vietminh activists and nationalists were detained and often mistreated. In the north, however, Ho Chi Minh and his colleagues retained considerable influence. The consolidation of these two opposing forces set the stage for the first Vietnam War, which lasted from 1946 until the French defeat in 1954. Conflict beckoned in Indonesia as well. British and Australian troops arrived soon after the Japanese surrender to pave the way for a return of Dutch authority and soon clashed with Indonesian nationalists who had no intention of accepting this. From Jakarta, Sukarno and his colleagues called for restraint, but civilians were not spared from the ongoing violence; indeed, some Dutch who had been interned by the Japanese returned to their camps, deeming these would be safer. Beginning in 1946 Dutch troops began a futile campaign to reclaim control, during which villages and towns suspected of harbouring militants were put to the torch. Finally, the Dutch relented and recognized Indonesia's independence in 1949.

The British also struggled to reassert their authority in their Southeast Asian colonies that had come under Japanese control. In Burma the nationalist leader Aung San switched from working with the Japanese to fighting alongside Britain in the final stages of the war. However, following the Japanese surrender, relations between the Burmese nationalists and the British quickly broke down. Though elements of the Burmese populace were initially glad to see the British drive out the Japanese, ongoing food shortages and inflation soon eroded that goodwill. Protests mounted; citing difficulties restraining some of his radical colleagues, Aung San demanded to know when Burma would achieve independence. He did not live to see the day, as he was assassinated in 1947, but his country achieved full sovereignty the following year. In Malaya, the struggle was more prolonged. The British aimed to reassert control over a territory where crime and ethnic conflicts between Malays and Chinese were on the rise and economic rebuilding posed a major challenge. At first, British plans were facilitated by the fact that the Communist-backed Malayan People's Anti-Japanese Army went along with London's request to demobilize. But by 1948, following a reneging of promised constitutional reforms, the Communists, still predominantly Chinese in membership, launched an insurrection that lasted for years, though by 1957 the British had largely quelled it and turned over power to an independent Malayan government. The Philippines, too, experienced significant unrest well after the war ended. After liberating the country from Japanese control, the United States granted formal independence in 1946 to a reliably pro-American Filipino government. The Communist-led Huk resistance movement initially disbanded after the Japanese surrender, but ongoing peasant discontent with a lack of land reform and difficult conditions led to a renewal of activity. The Huks attempted a general uprising against the pro-US government in 1950, though the action was ill-prepared and eventually crushed.

Thus, even in societies where Japanese control had been relatively short-lived the consequences were profound. For territories Japan had controlled for decades, such as Korea, the end of imperial rule in 1945 represented an even more radical break. At the time of the Japanese surrender, national-ist sentiment in the peninsula was intense, but so were social and political divisions nurtured by years of colonial rule. People's committees, formed throughout much of the country, provided basic services and order, but they also had social and political demands, notably for full Korean independ-ence, land redistribution, and the punishment of collaborators. This surge of popular activism was accompanied by the proclamation of a Korean People's Republic in the southern city of Seoul just days after the Japanese surrender, on 6 September 1945. The US State Department characterized the situation as follows: "Southern Korea can best be described as a powder keg ready to explode at the application of a spark.... All groups seem to have the common idea of seizing Japanese property, ejecting the Japanese from Korea, and achieving immediate independence. Beyond this they have few ideas. They are completely ripe for agitators."[24]

Despite the intensity of national feeling, emerging Cold War politics soon produced a divided Korea. At first, the Soviets and Americans agreed to share the occupation of the country. In December 1945 an international agreement promising Korea full independence within five years was signed. But the Soviet and US occupation regimes soon reflected these countries' sharp ideological differences. In the north the Soviets supported a transition from a broader ruling coalition to one dominated by Korean Communists, led by Kim Il-Sung. As early as 1946 land redistribution was underway, and before long press censorship and the persecution of political opponents and Christians intensified. In the south, events followed a very different course. Worried that social radicalism would encourage the rise of Communism, the Americans aligned with conservative elites. Some of the latter, notably future South Korean leader Syngman Rhee, were returning exiles, but oth-ers had worked with the Japanese for years. Opposition to the conservative trend in South Korean politics soon led to unrest; in 1948 violence erupted on the island of Cheju, and soon afterwards in the port city of Yŏsu. The South Korean security services, which included former agents of the Japanese, ruthlessly suppressed these rebellions, citing the need to quash Communism in Korea.

In 1948 the division of Korea was confirmed, with supporters of Rhee coming out ahead in UN-sponsored elections that were intended to include all Korea but that were boycotted by the Communists. The Republic of Korea was proclaimed on 15 August 1948; the Democratic People's Republic of Korea was established on 9 September. However, both Rhee and Kim hoped to unify Korea under their leadership, and within two years Kim attacked the South to achieve this goal. Koreans on both sides of the 38th parallel soon found themselves traumatized by war again.

For China, too, Japanese occupation proved divisive and destructive, especially in the northern regions of the country. Following the Japanese surrender Jiang Jieshi's GMD regime reasserted control over about 80 per cent of the country, including the major cities. But the Communists had a strong presence in the north, where Mao's CCP benefited from the Soviet invasion and short-term occupation of Manchuria. While Stalin formally turned over control of Chinese territory to the GMD, the Soviet Red Army handed over supplies and weapons to the Communists. For its part, the United States continued to assist Jiang during this period, while trying to avert a renewal of the Communist-Nationalist internal conflict by brokering negotiations between the two sides. By 1946 these talks had failed, however, and the CCP and GMD now engaged in a fight to the finish—the Chinese Civil War.

During this war aspects of the GMD's past came back to haunt it. Jiang and his supporters were initially able to reoccupy much of China, but their presence was often superficial. They relied upon some dubious allies, including former collaborators and, in some cases, stranded Japanese forces. In the cities many GMD officials engaged in corrupt practices. In the vast countryside the government tended to rely upon resented and discredited local elites. Jiang recognized there were problems; his regime courted workers, promised significant land reform to peasants, and engaged in some anti-bandit campaigns. But the reforms were largely unrealized, and by 1947 runaway inflation eroded already tenuous living standards. A demoralized, fragmented GMD was poorly prepared to face Communist offensives launched the following year.

The CCP's growing support—derived heavily but by no means exclusively from the countryside—did not come without challenges. During the war of resistance to Japan, the party had adapted its program of social and political reform to diverse regions and changing circumstances, and it now continued to do so. Anxious to build a broad support base, the CCP initially pursued a moderate course in dealing with "rich peasants" and local gentry, but in 1946–47 Mao and his colleagues encouraged a more radical approach. There was a political dimension to some of this, insofar as those who had worked with the Japanese were often singled out, but the primary aims of increasingly aggressive rent reductions and property confiscations were to gain support among "poorer" peasants for the CCP and to transform social relations in the villages. The process was often violent, with landlords being tortured in order to reveal the extent of their holdings. Those who came out on the losing end of the redistribution process—not all of whom were wealthy—often became pariahs and were driven from the village or even starved to death. By 1948 the party relented, concerned that it might alienate too many landlords and peasants who until recently had been willing to cooperate. This evolving strategy paid off. By the spring of 1947 the CCP had boosted its membership to about 2.7 members from 1.2 million two years earlier; it would reach nearly 4.5 million by the end of the Civil War in 1949. It consolidated its position in the north, went on the offensive in Manchuria, and eventually drove Jiang and his supporters off the mainland. Mao and his supporters proclaimed the People's Republic of China on 1 October 1949, while Jiang established a GMD-dominated regime on Taiwan.

Historian Joseph Esherick makes a strong case that a number of wartime social and cultural changes had ultimately worked to the Communists' advantage.[25] Though the GMD tried to mobilize Chinese nationalist sentiment against Japan, Mao and the CCP did a better job of channelling it. The Communists benefited from a rising tide of popular activism and a shift in cultural mores. Growing numbers of students asserted their autonomy from their elders and professors, stressing their identification with the common people and their commitment to change. Chinese women moved to the cities in unprecedented numbers, and these urban women were more inclined to break with traditional values. The popular culture of the day emphasized both national self-assertion and the rejection of traditional and wealth-based social hierarchies. Popular films cast the rich as decadent, westernized, and un-deserving, while stressing the virtuousness of the poor. One such movie, *Spring Dreams of Heaven*, featured one of its protagonists, a long-suffering mother, declaring, "The good suffer, the evil prosper! What kind of times are these?"[26] Though the film was, ironically, the product of a GMD government-run studio, it reflected more general aspirations to restrict, even punish, the rich and reward the poor. Given its identification with traditional elites and reputation for corruption, many Chinese hesitated to believe that the GMD could enact meaningful reform.

The CCP's victory derived not only from military prowess but also from identifying more effectively with demands for change. That said, many elements of the aforementioned popular activism were independent of the party or did not match its political priorities. Communist rural reforms might encourage village women to attend meetings and assert themselves, but gender issues were often subordinated to the class struggle. Substantial numbers of student activists shared the Communist dream of a regenerated, more socially just China and criticized the GMD, but the CCP increasingly asserted rigid control over the student movement. From 1949 onwards the Communist regime continued to discipline popular activism and silence dissenting views.

Conclusion: The Second World War in Perspective

Notwithstanding the dates that serve as the markers for public memory today—6 June 1944 (D-Day), 8 May 1945 (VE-Day), 6 August 1945 (Hiroshima), 15 August 1945 (Japan's surrender), 2 September 1945 (the final end of hostilities)—the Second World War did not end tidily. In East Asia struggles between recalcitrant imperial powers and local nationalists broke out. Civil war erupted in China, followed by Korea. There was fighting between different religious and ethnic communities in India, Burma, and Malaya. In Europe, there was civil war in Greece and severe political and ethnic strife in the East. The strength of nationalist opposition to European imperial rule was increasingly evident in the Middle East and Africa. West European nations experienced polarizing politics and often bitter labour disputes.

Despite these upheavals, the Allies, and more generally the international community, made various efforts to highlight the extent of atrocities against civilians during the war in both Europe and Asia. The Allies established the International Military Tribunal to conduct major war crimes cases. Twenty-two key Nazis were tried at Nuremberg between November 1945 and October 1946 on charges that included conspiracy to wage war, crimes against peace, war crimes, and crimes against humanity. Eleven of them were sentenced to death, while most of the remainder received various sentences. In Asia, the International Military Tribunal for the Far East put 25 key Japanese leaders on trial between 1946 and 1948; seven were subsequently executed. Many more trials would take place in the years that followed. The work of the first tribunals in Nuremberg and Tokyo was controversial at the time, because they were conducted by the victor powers, whose own wartime conduct was not examined, and because there were some key omissions on political grounds. For instance, the Emperor of Japan was exempted from prosecution because he was deemed crucial to the smooth functioning of the occupation.

Despite such controversies, the trials have had a lasting effect on international law, notably in the development and acceptance of the concept of "crimes against humanity," which involves atrocities such as the mass murder, enslavement, and deportation of populations. The countless instances of atrocities against civilians during the Second World War were also instrumental in the development of the 1949 Geneva Conventions, notably the Fourth Convention pertaining to the treatment of civilians under military occupation. It sets standards for humane treatment of civilians by occupation authorities, restricts forced labour and the transfer of populations, and prohibits pillaging and the collective punishment of non-combatants; in particular it emphasizes the requirement to treat children humanely. To be sure, just as the punishment of Axis leaders after the war has not ended crimes against humanity, the Geneva Conventions have not ended the mistreatment of civilians. However, the existence of the Conventions attest to how profoundly the civilian experiences of the Second World War have affected the norms of global society.

Significant though these concepts and conventions proved to be in the long run, they were too abstract, and too late, for those who had endured Nazi camps, Japanese detention centres, or prolonged internment in the Soviet GULAG. Their return to bodily health and mental well-being was often very difficult and sometimes impossible. Even for those who returned to their loved ones and to relatively stable and prosperous societies, the road ahead was not easy. Demobilized soldiers could not always shake off what they had seen. Children did not warm to, or sometimes even recognize, their fathers. Women who had found wartime service or circumstances energizing did not always find a shift to domestic life satisfying or even tolerable. Even in democratic states where freedom of speech and the rule of law were well-entrenched, members of ethnic minorities still wondered if the rhetoric of the wartime crusade for freedom and equality would have meaningful consequences for their own lives. And yet, for many the war years were experienced, or at least looked back upon, as an era of purpose, solidarity, and fulfillment. The various experiences of civilian mobilization examined in this book show that commitment and endurance abounded, though sometimes in the service of frightful causes.

The Second World War had unleashed powerful desires for retribution *and* hopes for building a better world, though what constituted such a world occasioned fierce differences. Yet many of those who experienced the conflict also wanted to escape memories of upheaval and destruction and move forward, whether that meant restoring families and friendships, finding new homes, or rebuilding shattered communities. The extent to which such competing goals were realized varied greatly. In the capitalist democracies of Western Europe and North America the postwar era was characterized by surprising prosperity, but also Cold War mobilization and sometimes a belief that the promise of equality could have been more completely fulfilled. The peoples of the Soviet Union experienced great hardships and found themselves subjected to renewed demands and restrictions. In Eastern Europe, Soviet power forged a new political order, facilitated by upheavals associated with the war; in China the impact of the Japanese invasion made it far more possible for the CCP to establish a new system as well. Throughout East Asia the war had stimulated mass nationalism and calls for remaking society. The weakening of European imperialism was also palpable in South Asia, the Middle East, and Africa. In sum, despite the desires of many governments and ordinary people to "regain" stability, this global conflict had wrought changes that could not be undone and was therefore one of the defining moments of modern world history.

Further Reading

Christopher Thorne, *The Far Eastern War: States and Societies 1941–1945* (London: Unwin Paperbacks, 1986) contains valuable comparisons. Yasmin Khan, *The Great Partition: The Making of India and Pakistan* (New Haven, CT: Yale University Press, 2007) captures the turmoil of the postwar years; William Cleveland, *A History of the Modern Middle East,* 3rd ed. (Boulder, CO: Westview Press, 2004) provides a clear discussion of developments in the region. For the United States, in addition to the books listed in Chapter 1, see Michael Adams, *The Best War Ever: America and World War II* (Baltimore, MD: Johns Hopkins University Press, 1994) and Lewis Erenberg and Susan Hirsch, eds., *The War in American Culture: Society and Consciousness during World War II* (Chicago, IL: University of Chicago Press, 1996). For the early postwar Soviet Union, see Elena Zubkova, *Russia after the War: Hopes, Illusions, and Disappointments, 1945–1957,* trans. Hugh Ragsdale (Armonk, NY: M.E. Sharpe, 1998); the essays in Susan Linz, ed., *The Impact of World War II on the Soviet Union* (Totowa, NJ: Rowman and Allanheld, 1985); Catherine Merridale, *Ivan's War: The Red Army 1939–1945* (London: Faber and Faber, 2005); and Amir Weiner, *Making Sense of War: The Second World War and the Fate of the Bolshevik Revolution* (Princeton, NJ: Princeton University Press, 2001).

On conditions in postwar Europe, see the opening chapters of Tony Judt, *Postwar: A History of Europe Since 1945* (London: Allen Lane, 2005). The essays in Richard Bessel and Dirk Schumann, eds., *Life After Death: Approaches to a Cultural and Social History of Europe during the 1940s and 1950s* (Cambridge: Cambridge University Press, 2003) and Monica Riera and Gavin Schaffer, eds., *The Lasting War: Society and Identity in Britain, France, and Germany after 1945* (New York: Palgrave Macmillan, 2008) provide additional perspectives. On expulsions, see Philipp Ther and Ana Siljak, eds., *Redrawing Nations: Ethnic Cleansing in East-Central Europe, 1944–1948* (Lanham, MD: Rowman and Littlefield, 2001). Bradley Abrams, "The Second World War and the East European Revolution," *East European Politics and Societies* 16 (2002): 623–64 is stimulating. For the rise of Communism in the region, see Norman Naimark and Leonid Gabianskii, eds., *The Establishment of Communist Regimes in Eastern Europe, 1944–1949* (Boulder, CO: Westview Press, 1997). Padraic Kenney, *Rebuilding Poland: Workers and Communists, 1945–1950* (Ithaca, NY: Cornell University Press, 1997) provides a detailed case study.

For Japan, see John Dower's excellent *Embracing Defeat: Japan in the Wake of World War II* (New York: W.W. Norton/The New Press, 1999). For the upheavals in East and Southeast Asia following the Japanese defeat, see Ronald Spector, *In the Ruins of Empire: The Japanese Surrender and the Battle for Postwar Asia* (New York: Random House, 2007) and Christopher Bayly and Tim Harper, *Forgotten Wars: The End of Britain's Asian Empire* (London: Allen Lane, 2007). For China, see Odd Arne Westad, *Decisive Encounters: The Chinese Civil War, 1946–1950* (Stanford, CA: Stanford University Press, 2003). Joseph Esherick, "War and Revolution: Chinese Society during the 1940s," *Twentieth-Century China* 27 (2001): 1–37 examines the broader structural changes at work. On the evolution of international law in the wake of the Second World War, see Geoffrey Best, *War and Law since 1945* (Oxford: Clarendon Press, 1994).

Notes

1 Quoted in Gardiner, *Wartime Britain*, 663.
2 Quoted in Mackay, *Test of War*, 225–26.
3 Quoted in Jeffrey Keshen, *Saints, Sinners, and Soldiers: Canada's Second World War* (Vancouver, BC: University of British Columbia Press, 2004), 269.
4 Quoted in Yasmin Khan, *The Great Partition: The Making of India and Pakistan* (New Haven, CT: Yale University Press, 2007), 27.
5 Quoted in Shirley Ann Wilson Moore, "Traditions from Home: African Americans in Wartime Richmond, California," in Lewis Erenberg and Susan Hirsch, eds., *The War in American Culture: Society and Consciousness during World War II* (Chicago, IL: University of Chicago Press, 1996), 276–77.
6 Quoted in Elaine Tyler May, "Rosie the Riveter Gets Married," in Erenberg and Hirsch, eds., *The War in American Culture*, 140.

7   Quoted in Rose, *Myth and the Greatest Generation*, 228.

8   See Studs Terkel, *"The Good War": An Oral History of World War Two* (New York: Pantheon, 1984), 131.

9   Quoted in Rose, *Myth and the Greatest Generation*, 237.

10 Quoted in Catherine Merridale, *Ivan's War: The Red Army 1939–1945* (London: Faber and Faber, 2005), 319.

11 Quoted in Elena Zubkova, *Russia after the War: Hopes, Illusions, and Disappointments, 1945–1957*, trans. Hugh Ragsdale (Armonk, NY: M.E. Sharpe, 1998), 38.

12 Quoted in Zubkova, *Russia after the War*, 32.

13 Quoted in Merridale, *Ivan's War*, 292.

14 Quoted in Zubkova, *Russia after the War*, 78.

15 See Sheila Fitzpatrick, "Postwar Soviet Society: The 'Return to Normalcy,' 1945–1953," in Susan Linz, ed., *The Impact of World War II on the Soviet Union* (Totowa, NJ: Rowman and Allanheld, 1985), 130.

16 Quoted in Bessel, *Germany 1945*, 312.

17 Quoted in Martin Gilbert, *The Day the War Ended: VE-Day 1945 in Europe and Around the World* (London: Harper Collins, 1995), 236.

18 Quoted in Jackson, *France: The Dark Years*, 592.

19 Quoted in Michael Wildt, "Continuities and Discontinuities of Consumer Mentality in West Germany in the 1950s," in Richard Bessel and Dirk Schumann, eds., *Life after Death: Approaches to a Cultural and Social History of Europe during the 1940s and 1950s* (Cambridge: Cambridge University Press, 2003), 211.

20 Quoted in Eagle Glassheim, "The Mechanics of Ethnic Cleansing: The Expulsion of Germans from Czechoslovakia, 1945–1947," in Philipp Ther and Ana Siljak, eds., *Redrawing Nations: Ethnic Cleansing in East-Central Europe, 1944–1948* (Lanham, MD: Rowman and Littlefield, 2001), 206.

21 See John Dower, *Embracing Defeat: Japan in the Wake of World War II* (New York: W.W. Norton/The New Press, 1999), 155–57.

22 Dower, *Embracing Defeat*, 30, 254–67.

23 Quoted in Ronald Spector, *In the Ruins of Empire: The Japanese Surrender and the Battle for Postwar Asia* (New York: Random House, 2007), 175.

24 Quoted in Bruce Cumings, *Korea's Place in the Sun: A Modern History* (New York: W.W. Norton, 1997), 192.

25 See his article, "War and Revolution: Chinese Society during the 1940s," *Twentieth-Century China* 27 (2001): 1–37.

26 Quoted in Esherick, "War and Revolution," 8.

Index